Being YOU is moST Definitely Cool

CHRISTOPHER CASTILE
with Susie Shellenberger

Publishers Since 1798

THOMAS NELSON PUBLISHERS
Nashville • Atlanta • London • Vancouver

Published in Nashville, Tennessee, by Thomas Nelson, Inc., and distributed in Canada by Word Communications, Ltd., Richmond, British Columbia, and in the United Kingdom by Word (UK), Ltd., Milton Keynes, England.

Library of Congress Cataloging-in-Publication Data

Castile, Chris.
    Being you is most definitely cool / Chris Castile with Susie Shellenberger.
        p.   cm.
    ISBN 0-7852-7826-5 (pbk.)
    1. Castile, Chris. 2. Christian biography—United States.
3. Teenagers—Religious life. 4. Actors—United States—Biography.
I. Shellenberger, Susie. II. Title.
BR1725.C33A3 1996
248.2'092—dc20
[B]   95–40375
                                             CIP
                                             AC

Printed in the United States of America

1 2 3 4 5 6 7 - 02 01 00 99 98 97 96

Dedication

Many thanks to my mom, Donna; my dad, Jon; and my sister, Bethany. Also to my Papa and Grandma Sanada. In addition, I would like to include Dan Wulken and Bob Seers.
You all helped shape me into who I am today.
I love you all!

Contents

Acknowledgments

Without these special people, this book would not have been possible:

- Susie Shellenberger
- Greg Johnson
- everyone at Thomas Nelson Publishers
- Cynthia Snyder
- Judy Savage
- everyone involved with *Beethoven, Beethoven's 2nd,* and *Step by Step*
- everyone involved with all the other projects I've been privileged to work on
- Attila Aszodi
- Amanda Llewellyn
- Steve S.

To all those I may have unintentionally failed to mention, please forgive my scattered teenage brain. You're all terrific!

A Note from Chris

. . . ▾

Not many teens my age do what I'm about to do, and certainly not many actors my age do this. The important feat? I'm going to take a risk. I'm choosing to open up and be really, really honest. To do that, I realize I have to make myself vulnerable. And in doing *that,* I take the risk that you might not like who I am. That's kind of scary, but I believe it's worth the chance. Why? Because real growth comes from daring to share what's inside.

So there they are . . . my fears, my beliefs, and the stuff in life I value. You may or may not agree with what I say, but that's not the issue. What's really at stake here is that you receive courage from my openness and honesty to take a deeper look at your own life. What do *you* believe? What do *you* value? And why?

I realize that speaking out about respect for the opposite sex, obeying your parents, and standing up for what you believe in are not real popular teen topics. But again, I'm risking popularity because there's something much deeper at stake. It's a thing called integrity. (Which isn't a hot topic in the locker room or the school cafeteria, right?) By choosing to be open about my own beliefs, I hope you'll receive hope and direction in your own journey toward adulthood.

Your Friend,
Chris Castile

It All Started When . . .

I've known that I wanted to act ever since I can remember. Really. I mean, I was into it even at age three. I'd dress up like certain personalities and walk around imitating people—trying to look and sound like them. I'd put on this little suit I had (complete with a clip-on tie) and stand in front of a plant stand that I used for a podium and give "speeches," trying to imitate President Reagan.

To me, he was President Ronald McReagan. I was crazy about Ronald McDonald, and since our president's first name was Ronald, in my mind that translated into Ronald McReagan!

I was so caught up in my imaginary world of being Ronald Reagan that I begged Mom to write him a letter for me. She finally agreed to do it, and she told him all about my "speeches" and how I was always trying to imitate him. You can imagine my excitement when I received a letter and photo from him! The photo was autographed. I still treasure that memento.

I was particularly fascinated with historical figures from the past, like George Washington and General Braddock. I dressed up like them and went around pretending I was them.

I had this set of interactive cassettes that were incredible! I had such a blast listening to them. I mean, these tapes had sound effects of horses and guns and stuff. They really sparked my imagination. I often pretended I was right in the middle of all the action. So, naturally, it was easy to make the action happen right around me. I fought battles, signed peace treaties, and rescued prisoners of war—all in my living room!

Well, I listened to these tapes so much that I actually memorized them. It got to the point that I didn't even have to *play* a tape; I could recite the entire thing!

Little Soldier

In all the pictures of the war, I had noticed almost all of the men's shirts had ruffles on them. So I asked my mom if she could make some ruffles on a white shirt. Then I asked if she could make a Revolutionary War outfit for me. So she made me a little red coat with gold buttons on the front.

I'd get all decked out in my white ruffled shirt and red coat and put on tube socks and pants that came to my knees. I'd try to look as "Revolutionary" as possible. Then I'd grab my toy gun and actually go around reciting and acting out the Revolutionary War.

Mom thought it was weird. Dad just laughed. I was really into it! We'd go to the grocery store, and I'd grab my gun and wipe out the people in the aisles and the checkout lines while reciting all this Revolutionary War stuff.

Mom didn't want to squelch my imagination, but she

also wanted to tame the show a bit. So she made me quit shooting at people and told me I could only shoot at the ground. I didn't like sports at the time, so she resigned herself to assuming this was my creative outlet. I was having a blast!

I also had this little notebook I carried around with me. I often scribbled in it and pretended it was the Constitution, while continuing to recite Revolutionary War facts.

People would look at me, turn around, and start talking. I *loved* the attention. And I also loved being someone else. Other times, I dressed up like a Viking, a professional baseball player, or some other personality. But I kept coming back to the Revolutionary War era because I was so fascinated with it.

Welcome to Independence Hall

A nearby city had a building that was a replica of Independence Hall. Mom and Dad thought it would be fun to take me there. Well, you can imagine how magnetized I became to that building! It was awesome. Everything looked so real. And of course, it really enhanced my little game of pretending.

My parents took me there frequently. It was never crowded. (How many preschool kids are fascinated with the Revolutionary War?) Usually the only visitors besides us were elderly people. Before we left our house, I'd dress up in my Revolutionary clothes. The costume and the building made that time period seem so real. I'd walk around the room pretending I was the president. I'd walk up to people, extend my hand, and exclaim how thrilled I was to have them in my home. Well, you can imagine how the older folks reacted. They thought it was adorable, and I began to realize that the more I pretended, the more affirmation I received.

▼ ▼ ▼ ▼ ▼

I'd walk around the room pretending I was the president. I'd walk up to people, extend my hand, and exclaim how thrilled I was to have them in my home.

I wasn't acting to get attention, but when I received it, I really enjoyed it. It didn't take much to get me hooked.

My Declaration!

After a few visits, Mom and Dad pretty much had the entire building memorized and didn't really want to keep going back, but they did, for me—I *loved* it. This was my fun! Most kids want to go to the park, swing, or play on the merry-go-round. I wanted to keep going back to this building.

The more I went, the more I'd add to my act. Soon I was taking local maps with me and pretending they were war maps. I even asked Mom to buy me some special paper—you know, that crinkly kind. As soon as I got my hands on that, I copied the entire Declaration of Independence on it. It felt like I was really living this period in time. Mom eventually bought me coins and some Revolutionary maps so I didn't have to pretend with local city maps anymore.

I always knew it was acting, though. Even though it *felt* like everything was real, I somehow understood the difference between fantasy and reality even at a young age.

From Soldier to Actor

Though I loved this particular period in time, I also enjoyed hearing about other historical personalities. Mom is a great reader, and she began reading to me when I was just six months old. She's told me that's probably why I had such a great vocabulary at a young age. I think all that reading really kindled my imagination. I watched TV, too, but my mom's reading to me enhanced my ability to dream up stuff—you know, pretend.

It also piqued *my* interest in reading. I guess when you really love something, the more you see others doing it, the more you want to do it. That's the way it was with books. The more I heard Mom and Dad read, the more I wanted to read. Mom used to be a preschool teacher, and she was thrilled that I wanted to learn at such an early age. So she worked with me, and I began reading at age five.

▼　▼　▼　▼　▼

It got to the point that every time we went out, I was someone different. I enjoyed coming up with a variety of personalities that I'd act out with costumes.

But back to the acting stuff—it got to the point that every time we went out, I was someone different. I enjoyed coming up with a variety of personalities that I'd act out with costumes. Captain Hook was a lot of fun. One of the advantages of living in Southern California is being near Disneyland. Every time we visited the park, I'd pick up a new accessory to use in my pretending games. For instance, one time I got a hat with *Captain Chris* embroidered on it. On another visit, I picked up a pirate map. Another time I got a sword—that was my favorite!

Well, you can imagine how much attention all this caused. It seemed like tons of people were coming up to Mom and saying, "He ought to be on TV." Or "Why don't you look into acting for him?" Of course, I was all for it! I literally begged Mom and Dad to let me act. And the more I heard people telling Mom to put me in show business, the more determined I became.

How It Happened

For four years, I couldn't think of anything else. It was all I talked about, day after day. Mom finally got tired of saying no, and even though she was leery about the whole thing, she started doing some checking around.

You know the old saying, "I have a friend who's a friend of a friend of a friend"? Mom didn't know anything about show biz, and though she was searching for information, she didn't really know what to ask or whom to talk to. But it just so happened that my grandpa had an acquaintance whose wife was an agent. He was just an acquaintance—not really even a friend. So it still seemed like a long shot. But one day in an ordinary conversation, this guy casually asked my grandpa if he had any grandchildren who were interested in acting. Grandpa's entire face lit up, and he told the gentleman all about me.

We were told to send some regular, everyday snapshots of me to the agent. The next thing we knew, the agent made an appointment to meet me. I remember Dad saying, "Chris, don't get your hopes up. Hundreds of kids want to be actors."

I met with the agent, recited a few lines, and did a cold reading (which means I had to read something I hadn't had time to rehearse). Then I left the room as she patted me on the back, saying, "Good, Chris." We were told that if the agent called back, she was interested. And if she didn't call back, I shouldn't be hurt but grateful I had even received the opportunity to meet with someone in the business.

▼ ▼ ▼ ▼ ▼

It had finally paid off. My dream was coming true at last!

The agent *did* call back—the very next day! She said that I had the kind of personality it took to make it in professional acting and she wanted to represent me.

I was seven years old. A lot of begging and several costume changes had been made in the past four years. But now it had finally paid off. My dream was coming true at last!

Lights, Camera, Action!

Now that I had an agent, it was time to get serious. The first thing I was asked to do was get professional photographs taken so I could create a composite. A composite is a packet of several different photos. It worked like this: From the photos we had taken, we selected one for an 8 x 10 enlargement. Then, on the back of that photo, we placed a variety of smaller shots that showed my versatility. For instance, one shot was of me looking into a microscope. In another photo, I looked surprised.

When agents are trying to line up work for their clients, they need to show the aspiring actor in as many different avenues as possible. So we tried to create a composite that would highlight my personality in a number of settings.

I feel like I'm a pretty versatile actor. I feel comfortable doing a variety of different roles. In other words, give me the description of the specific kind of character you want me to play, and I'll do it. I think it's *fun* to slip in and out of different types of characters. I did it so much as a pre-schooler that now it's an easy transition.

The first thing my agent did was set up several commercial auditions for me. She figured that even if I didn't get the job, the experience of just simply trying out would be beneficial.

By the time my first audition rolled around, though, I was missing a tooth. I was at that awkward stage where I was beginning to lose my baby teeth, and my permanent teeth were not all in. I looked pretty funny! I had one tooth that was sort of halfway there, you know?

It was then I began to learn that one of the most fun parts of show business is having access to props, which can make things that aren't really happening appear as if they are. And because commercials call for people with perfect teeth, I needed a prop. A Hollywood dentist fitted me for flippers—phony teeth. Now I looked like I had a perfect, full set of teeth whenever I smiled or opened my mouth wide.

It All Adds Up

We soon discovered how quickly the expenses can mount when you're trying to launch yourself into the business. At that time, for instance, a full set of flippers (top and bottom teeth) cost $200. It cost another $800 to take an essential step: joining SAG (Screen Actors Guild), a union that strives to maintain the actor's best interests and makes sure an actor is treated properly when on the set. We borrowed the money from an uncle of mine.

Now, an actor doesn't *have* to be a member of SAG to get work—there are a lot of nonunion jobs available. But the benefits for members are really big. For instance, you get health and dental insurance, a teacher on the set for all union jobs, and you gain the assurance of working on a safe set: Everything is checked out ahead of time by another union professional to ensure that everything is sturdy and free of potential physical hazards.

Well, finally the big day arrived—my first audition! It was for a McDonald's commercial. I remember going into a room with a bunch of important people—men and women with glasses and ponytails sitting around a table. They called in five children at a time, and we were given instructions on which character from a script we were to play. My role was "Jason."

We all read our lines and were then told to memorize them. A few minutes later, we handed back our scripts and acted from memory. After that, we heard "Good job" and were sent home. The whole thing took only ten minutes.

A few days later we learned that I had received a callback (another audition). This time, instead of bringing in five kids at a time, they only brought in two at a time. I went in with a little girl.

▼ ▼ ▼ ▼ ▼

I remember jumping up and down and phoning my grandpa and screaming, "Papa, I got the commercial! I got it!"

I received a third callback, auditioned again, and left. Mom was wearing a pager by now so we wouldn't miss any calls. We stopped at the grocery store, and since she hadn't been beeped, we assumed they were still auditioning people.

By the time we got home, though, there was a message on our answering machine saying I had gotten the job. Boy, was I excited! My first job. Even though it would be neat to make money, I was really more excited about the chance to be on TV.

I remember jumping up and down and phoning my grandpa and screaming, "Papa, I got the commercial! I got it! I wanna share my money with you!" I didn't even know how much money I'd get for a commercial. I was just so stoked about being able to make some money for the first time in my life, I wanted to share it with those around me.

The commercial was shot in an actual school setting. A group of kids stood near a chalkboard. The teacher was asking us several questions when we were interrupted by an announcer on the class intercom advertising the variety of items McDonald's had to offer. Then the cameras cut to an outside scene of a guy pulling up to the drive-thru. My job was to peek through a group of kids, flex my muscles, and smile.

In commercials, the scenes are usually shot in sequence. But once in a while, they aren't, and it's hard to tell how it's all going to fit together.

A Lot to Learn

I was new at this, though. Remember, this was my very first commercial. My first lesson came quickly. I didn't have a clue about directors and authority and stuff. So when the director approached me, explained what I was supposed to do, then asked, "Would you like to try that now?" I politely said, "No."

I honestly thought he wanted my opinion. I didn't realize he was simply trying to tell me in a nice way what was expected of me. During a break, Mom pulled me aside and explained that he was just trying to be diplomatic—that I was supposed to do whatever he asked.

It was a lot of fun, but it's actually a lot of work too. It gets tiring and people forget their lines, or they stand the wrong way, and everything has to be repeated so many times. For lunch, we all got to eat McDonald's food. I grabbed an Egg McMuffin. I felt really "grown up." My first job, getting an actual lunch break, earning money—I loved it!

Learning Isn't Always Fun!

Now that I actually had some professional experience under my belt, I was ready to go again! My agent didn't want me to get my hopes up, though. She said, "Chris, remember, there are hundreds of kids out there. And all of them are competing with you. You might go on fifty auditions and actually only get one. Just be patient."

It took some time, but I landed another commercial, this time for M&M's. It was set up like a birthday party, and I was supposed to be eating the colored candies while standing next to all the presents.

Again, because I was so young and so new to all of this, I didn't know that when filming food commercials, most actors don't actually swallow the food. They hold it in their mouths, and when the cameras are off, they spit it all out.

▼ ▼ ▼ ▼ ▼

Because I was so young and so new to all of this, I didn't know that when filming food commercials, most actors don't actually swallow the food.

See, they know a few hundred takes will go by before some directors finally feel they have what they want. Therefore, if they actually eat the food during each take, they'll not only weigh more than when they started the commercial, but they'll be pretty sick as well.

I *loved* M&M's, and because I wasn't allowed to have much candy when I was young, I was pretty excited about eating them and getting paid for it. To me, it was a dream come true! I was in candy heaven. So I was actually *eating* the product during each take. Well, they had tons of candy available because, of course, we'd take hundreds of shots. Since M&M's were one of my favorite munchies, I wasn't embarrassed about asking if I could even eat between takes. They didn't care.

I was stuffing myself and having the time of my life! I couldn't believe my good fortune—all the M&M's I wanted. I literally ate them by the handful for hours on end. Could life get any better? I *loved* show biz!

We finally finished the commercial, and Mom and I headed home. The next morning I was itching like crazy. I couldn't figure it out. No matter how much I scratched, I continued to itch. When I took off my pajama shirt, Mom almost screamed. My back was covered with welts! I'd eaten so many M&M's my body had reacted to having too much sugar in my system, and I broke out in hives. After getting an injection, I decided I was finished with M&M's for a while. To this day, I still can't eat very many of them. I eat a few in moderation (my favorites are peanut M&M's), but I learned my lesson on overdoing it with candy!

Still Learning . . .

Remember, I was seven years old, and I was going to public school. I guess a lot of kids would tell their friends during recess that they'd just shot a commercial. But I wanted to make sure that my classmates wouldn't treat me weird or look at me differently. So I tried to keep the whole thing secret . . . until my peers finally recognized me on TV. Then the word was out!

▼ ▼ ▼ ▼ ▼

I wanted to make sure that my classmates wouldn't treat me weird. So I tried to keep the whole thing secret . . . until my peers finally recognized me on TV.

At first, they thought it was cool. But after a while, it became a little uncomfortable. They'd ask me why I wasn't wearing Reeboks or some other expensive item. "You probably make all kinds of money," they'd say. "So how come you don't wear the best stuff?" It was hard. Kids would come up and just kick me or hit me—for no reason. Maybe they were jealous, or maybe they just assumed I thought I was cool since I was on TV. Nothing could have been farther from the truth!

During the next few years, I continued doing commercials and loved it. In fact, that's all I really wanted to do. Television and movies never entered my mind. I was happy just shooting a few commercials every now and then.

Mom and Dad felt if I was going to act, though, I ought to be as good as I could be. By this time they were convinced that I had raw talent, but they were also wondering what could happen if my raw talent was trained—just how much potential did I have? We'd never know unless I took acting lessons and learned how to develop my natural ability.

I really enjoyed the classes. I was challenged to dig way down inside myself and come up with stuff I didn't even know I had. Sometimes I'd have to be angry—explosively angry. Other times I'd have to laugh hysterically and make it seem real. Or I'd have to cry. It was a great experience because it showed me things about myself and my ability that I would never have thought to rely on. My coach taught me a variety of methods for getting into a multitude of different characters.

I also learned improvisation. That's where the teacher will give you a situation and you act on it. You create on the spot how you'll complete the scene. Your dialogue, your character—everything has to be thought up and acted out on the spot! It taught me how to think and produce in a variety of situations.

We were also taught scene study. That's where you're given a script to take home with you. We were instructed to study and memorize it overnight. The next day, we'd act with the other kids in the class without scripts.

In another acting class I took, our coach produced a showcase at the end of the semester. It was a small show that demonstrated what his students had learned and what they could do. We'd be performing comedy and drama in an array of sketches and vignettes. We knew that several agents and casting directors would be in the audience. I really wasn't nervous; I was anxious. I couldn't wait to take the stage and come to life.

Well, afterward, several agents began asking my coach questions. "Who *is* this kid?" And "Why haven't we seen him on interviews for TV or movies?"

My agent finally felt I was ready to begin auditioning for things beyond commercials. By this time I was confident and had learned the necessary tools I would need for a role longer than a commercial spot. I was ready for television!

Brighter Lights

The very first television role I landed was with the ABC sitcom *The Wonder Years*. This show was set in the '60s and centered around Kevin Arnold—a young teen coming of age. It was a top-rated show and had done consistently well over the years, so I was pretty excited. I played the role of Kevin as a younger boy. I wasn't actually on screen; only my voice was used. It was called "looping."

I sat in a studio and watched Kevin (Fred Savage) on a gigantic screen. I had to study his moving mouth, and at a specific time, I read lines. In other words, I was Kevin's voice at a younger age.

It's really fascinating how this whole looping process works. As I watched the movements of his mouth on screen, a light indicator appeared with numbers just below the screen to cue the technicians exactly where to put my voice. They played the scene with the sound up to the part where I began speaking. I watched Kevin and the blinking light while listening to the scene. Right before I was to begin speaking, the light would blink three times. On the fourth blink, I delivered my lines while continuing to watch his mouth so I could speak in tempo with his movements.

▼　▼　▼　▼　▼

My next television appearance was on another sitcom called My Two Dads. That's where I met Staci Keanan.

My next television appearance was on another sitcom called *My Two Dads*. That's where I met Staci Keanan, who's now one of my older sisters in my *Step by Step* family. The story line centered around a young teen girl (Staci) whose mother had died. Her mom had two very close male friends (Greg Evigan and Paul Reiser) whom she had asked to look after her daughter in the event that she should die.

The two men rented an apartment in the same building as the judge who appointed them guardians during the reading of the mother's will. Thus, the teen girl had two dads and a neighborly judge who would look in on them from time to time.

I played the role of Truman. He was a real intellectual kid who met Staci in a cafe and was simply awestruck by her—one of those "love at first sight" things. Only the feeling wasn't mutual. I followed her around the entire show. She kept trying to get rid of me, and I kept hanging on. My last scene in the show was when I grabbed her hands and proceeded to drag her out the door while she screamed, "I don't want to go to Aruba!" It was a blast. I loved working with Staci. She's a lot of fun and a real pro. I knew I'd enjoy working with her again.

After that appearance, I landed a role on *Hurricane Sam*. This never actually became a show. By that I mean it aired once or twice and that's all. It was shot as a pilot, which means it hadn't actually been picked up by a network yet. If a pilot *is* picked up by a network, it will be scheduled into their regular lineup of shows and may then possibly film thirteen to twenty-four episodes. Hundreds of pilots are shot each year. And as you can tell by glancing at *TV Guide,* only a few make it into the fall or replacement schedule.

Even though *Hurricane Sam* wasn't picked up, I was still grateful for the work. It gave me more needed experience and again, I had the privilege of working with some terrific people. It starred Fran Drescher (who's now on *The Nanny*) and Ben Savage (who now stars on *Boy Meets World).* Fran played my mom, and I was the nerdy next-door neighbor to Ben.

Another pilot I guested on was *Daphne.* This was never even aired. It was a pilot shot for Aaron Spelling. At that time, UCLA film students at the extension campus received financial funding from Mr. Spelling to create presentation pilots. He'd set aside a specific time to view their pilots and decide whether or not he wanted to use any of them for future shows. Again, it was good acting experience for me, so I'm thankful for the opportunity.

Even though I had a few commercials under my belt, I was still considered someone who was trying to get started. Therefore, I figured the more I did (whether it actually aired or not) was to my benefit. I was filling up my résumé with a steady stream of work. This would later prove to directors and producers that I could handle the challenge of sitcom acting and working at a fast pace.

It Gets Better

▾ ▾ ▾ ▾ ▾

Because I was picking up some great experience, I was feeling more confident and anxious to try a variety of roles.

Because I was picking up some great experience, I was

feeling more confident and anxious to try a variety of roles. I soon landed a guest appearance on the NBC sitcom *Empty Nest*. I played the role of "Larry," who was just a regular kid. This was a welcome reprieve from the intellectual or nerd roles. Larry was afraid of the dark, and to help me get over this fear, Dr. Weston (Richard Mulligan) and Nurse Laverne Todd (Park Overall) gave me a stuffed fox to hug. The fun part was that after the show, they let me keep it. It's a neat reminder of my time spent on *Empty Nest*. The cast was terrific and very complimentary. We all got along great.

A few years later, I landed another guest role on this show. I was excited to go back since I'd had such a fun time with the cast earlier. It also felt good to walk into a familiar situation. The cast was also excited about it and kept telling me how much I'd grown since the last time we were together.

This time I played comedian Jack Carter's grandson. My name was Barry, and I told jokes constantly—imitating Jack's delivery. I had a blast doing this one!

It wasn't long afterward that I landed a role on *American Dreamer* and worked with Robert Urich. I appeared in a dream as an anesthesiologist, which meant I got to walk into surgery wearing greens. It was really fun and different from anything I'd played up to this point. Me—a doctor? I loved it!

When I was cast as a costar in *The Fanelli Boys,* I played the part of Timmy, who had a broken leg. Robert Stack, who hosts *Unsolved Mysteries,* was the guest star of this sitcom. Since I had a broken leg, I spent the entire episode in a wheelchair. Again, it was a different role for me, and one that I enjoyed. I learned how to pop wheelies on that show! The cast—Joe Pantoliano, Ann Gilbert, Christopher Meloni, Ned Eisenberg, Andy Hirsch, and Richard Libertini—was terrific. They were great guys to work with, and they treated me like we'd known each other forever.

The Experience Adds Up

When I was cast as a guest on *The Family Man* (starring Gregory Harrison and Scott Weinger), it was really a surprise. I had actually auditioned for a different role on another series. The casting director told me I just wasn't right for that particular role. And then she said, "I like your talent, though, and I'll remember you for something else. Hang in there. I'll be calling you."

▼ ▼ ▼ ▼ ▼

Directors and producers were now starting to recognize me. The variety of work I'd been doing was finally starting to matter.

Well, it just so happened that she also worked on *The Family Man,* and called me one day saying, "I didn't forget. Are you ready to act?" I played Lowell Pennington on this particular show. Gregory Harrison (the dad) had agreed to switch roles with his son for one day. It was really a funny show. Because the dad was suddenly left with the responsibility of doing his son's homework, he found himself right in the middle of a stack of algebra. That's where I came in. I played a math whiz who came over to tutor Gregory Harrison with the mountain of unfinished math.

To a small degree, directors and producers were now starting to recognize me. The variety of work I'd been doing was finally starting to matter. I won the role of host for an ABC special entitled *Money Made Easy.*

Some of the same producers from *Family Man* were also working on a sitcom pilot called *Going Places.* Since I had worked for a few of these guys before, they remembered me when I auditioned for a guest role on their show.

I originally went in for only one appearance on one

show. I played Sam. Afterward, the producers asked me to come back for four more episodes. I was really jazzed. And after my fifth guest appearance on this show, they asked me to join the cast as a regular! At this point we weren't sure if the show was actually going to be scheduled in the regular lineup or not. Before we knew whether or not *Going Places* would make it, the producers asked if they could "hold" me for something else in case we didn't make the lineup.

The bad news was that *Going Places* never gained an audience; therefore, I lost my chance to become a regular cast member. But the good news is that some of those producers went on to produce another ABC sitcom called *Step by Step*. And you guessed it! The "something else" they wanted to hold me for was the role of Mark Foster on *Step*.

The Big
Screen!

Before I actually started filming *Step by Step,* I interviewed for a role in the movie *Beethoven.* This was a real leap for me because I didn't have any movie experience. And even though I was being held for the new ABC sitcom with Patrick Duffy and Suzanne Somers, it was still a big question mark in all of our minds. At that early stage in the game, we all knew it could end up like a hundred other sitcoms: never picked up past the pilot stage, or picked up and run for only a year. And since we hadn't begun filming yet, I still didn't have any experience as a regular cast member.

I wanted this shot, though. I mean, why not go for all you can? I'd never know if I was capable of doing a full-length movie unless I tried, right? I was ten years old at the time. Mom drove me to the interview, and then, as usual, I walked into the audition alone.

I was in a room with the director and two of the producers. I sat with them at a big table and was handed a portion of the script that contained the character Ted Newton's lines. Even though I'd never been cast in a movie before, I had done a few silver screen auditions. I felt relaxed.

I began reading Ted's lines. It seemed like a really fun script, and I fell in love with the character and the whole story immediately. At the conclusion of the interview, I left feeling pretty good about myself. I had given it 100 percent, and I thought I did well.

▾ ▾ ▾ ▾ ▾

You're only called for a screen test when they're really serious about you.

A few days later I was called in for a screen test. I knew then that I had a good chance of getting the part. You're only called for a screen test when they're really serious about you. A screen test means that you're put on videotape. It gives the producers and director a chance to watch you over and over. There are usually a handful of actors brought in for this test, and all of them have made it to the "finals," so to speak. So even with a screen test, there's still quite a bit of competition, but at least you have the satisfaction of knowing you're in the final running.

Celebration!

It wasn't long after the screen test that I received the news that I'd been cast as Ted Newton in *Beethoven!* I'd won the part. My first movie! I was so excited, I could hardly stand it. I was especially jazzed about getting to be in such a *fun* movie. I love animals, and I was really looking forward to working with the dogs.

The other two kids who were cast—Nicholle Tom (who's currently on *The Nanny* and played my older sister Ryce Newton) and Sarah Rose Karr (who played in *Kindergarten Cop* and was cast as my younger sister Emily)—were also excited about working with animals. Sarah was especially excited about it because she had never even held a puppy before she began this film!

We began filming in March. When all three kids had been hired, they took us to meet Beethoven. I had to walk with him because they wanted to see if I could control him and if he was afraid of me.

Him afraid of *me?* I don't think so. That dog was huge! He weighed 185 pounds, and at that time (remember, I was twelve years old), I only weighed 75 pounds. This dog was over one hundred pounds heavier than I was! When he stood on his hind legs, he was even taller than me! But Beethoven and I got along great. Even though he's gigantic, he's really a baby at heart—just one big gentle dog. But working with such a large animal can sometimes be pretty funny!

The *Real* Star

In one of my first scenes, I was supposed to walk down the street with Beethoven. Well, we got down the street all right . . . but not the way I'd planned! I was standing there letting Beethoven sniff a tree, and the next thing I knew I was flying down the street! Since he was so much heavier than I was, I ended up going with him. The trainer called him, and off he went—with me still attached to his leash! As he dragged me down the street, I was literally doing belly flops on the cement! I skidded across the concrete scratching up my arms and legs and tearing my clothes. But Beethoven was such a softy, I couldn't help but hug him . . . even when things didn't go as planned.

In another scene, Beethoven was supposed to go to the bathroom. The script called for him to sniff quickly, then go. He sniffed all right. He sniffed and sniffed and sniffed. And he *kept* sniffing! It was hilarious. We were all standing around going, "Hurry up! Just use the bathroom!"

In one of my other scenes, I was being chased by bullies. Here we were, filming in Pasadena, California, on a super-hot day. It was 110 degrees, and I was wearing a *sweater*. I was sweating like crazy and felt like I was dying. Then I glanced around . . . and there was Beethoven standing under a big air conditioner waiting for his part. I couldn't help but laugh. We all knew who the *real* star was!

▼ ▼ ▼ ▼ ▼

There was Beethoven standing under a big air conditioner waiting for his part. I couldn't help but laugh. We all knew who the real star was!

One of the fun things about Beethoven's star status was that he didn't have to make all the rehearsals. We had a huge stuffed animal that was used as a stand-in. We acted and reacted around the fake animal, so when the *real* dog was brought in, we were ready. The prop guys made it really fun to work with this stand-in. They'd dress him up and put different things on him, like a hat, sweater, or a funny nose. One time he was even wearing glasses!

It's Not Always What It Looks Like

The fun thing about film is that you can cheat. In other words, things aren't always exactly as they seem. I'm told that back in the days of black and white television, they often used Hershey's syrup for blood. If you think about it, it really *would* look like blood if everything was in black and white.

Even though it looked like Dr. Varnick (the evil veterinarian) was really bleeding when he was bitten by Beethoven, it wasn't real blood. Hollywood has a way of making everything look real! Fake blood (or stage blood) is often used, and on film it looks exactly like the real thing.

And remember the scene toward the end of the movie when I'm driving into the pet supply building? The car's front bumper slammed into a table holding several syringes. The needles went flying through the air and all landed on Dr. Varnick's chest. Well . . . not *exactly*. But it sure *looked* like that's what happened! How it actually happened is one of those Hollywood secrets I can't reveal.

One of my favorite scenes in this movie is the one I just mentioned—when I get to drive the car and smash into the pet supply building. In the film, it looks like I'm flooring it and going in at a pretty good speed, doesn't it? The truth is, I only got to drive about two inches. The rest of the time, the car was in neutral and I was merely holding the vehicle while a tow truck pulled us forward. A stunt man who was my height, dressed like me, and wore a wig to match my hair drove the car when it went over the curb.

Even though it looked like I did a great job of crashing into the building, sending huge pieces of wood flying everywhere, I can't actually take credit for knocking down a wooden wall. This building wasn't even made out of actual wood. It looked like real wood—and even appeared to be very heavy—but it was really light as a feather. It's a special kind of wood that's used in almost every smash scene you'll see on film or on TV. It's called balsa wood. It floats (like most wood), and it doesn't take any strength at all to break it.

I'm sure you remember the funny scene when the Newton family is having a cookout and Brad and Brie are trying to get George to sign a contract. Beethoven flies across the yard like a huge airplane dragging Brad and Brie with him. It's hilarious! These two are sitting in lawn chairs one second, and the next thing they know, they're scooting all over the place—while still in their chairs!

Here's what *really* happened: Beethoven simply pulled on the table when no one was around. After that was captured on film, the two chairs were connected to a tractor and dragged around in a huge, open field. Everything else was added and mixed later.

My hair is naturally blond, but the hair stylist dyed it brown every day to match Charles Grodin's (Mr. Newton's). It wasn't a permanent dye, that's why we had to keep reapplying it on a daily basis. I came in early, and they'd wash it into my hair. At night, I'd wash it out. A few times the script called for me to run through the sprinkler. Because the dye in my hair was washable, we couldn't keep it from running down my face. It was pretty funny! I'd run through the sprinkler with brown streaks covering my cheeks. The makeup personnel had to keep blotting it up.

(Sarah Rose enjoyed the water scene but didn't enjoy waiting to dry off. After shooting the sprinkler sequence she said, "I want a fur coat like Beethoven, so I won't be cold when they turn on the water.")

In another scene, I was supposed to be crying in my bedroom. In real life, though, it was my birthday! Some of the crew members had brought in a big, scrumptious cake and had given me some baseball cards I'd been wanting. So naturally I was really excited . . . yet there I was lying on my bed and supposed to be looking sad. It was really hard, but I finally managed to forget my birthday for a while, and I pulled it off.

Step by Step

We finished filming *Beethoven* in July, and *Step by Step* began production a few days later. It felt great to finally be a part of a regular cast family and to have a consistent role. We signed a seven-year contract and began as part of the fall 1991 T.G.I.F. (Thank Goodness It's Funny) lineup. We originally followed the ABC sitcom *Family Matters*. A couple of years later, we remained on the T.G.I.F. schedule but followed *Boy Meets World*.

Life on the Set

Being on a weekly sitcom is a blast. I love it! But it's also a lot of work. We actually go through four versions of the same script each week, so an actor can get real used to his lines, perfect just the right voice inflection, and suddenly be handed an entirely different version of the script. Producers can change a script at a moment's notice if they don't like it. Cast members have to always be ready to adapt. The good part of all this is the fact that the producers have the show's best interest at heart. I mean, they want our show to be successful even more than we do. So when a change is made, I realize it's for the benefit of the show at large.

▼ ▼ ▼ ▼ ▼

Being on a weekly sitcom is a blast. I love it! But it's also a lot of work.

Learning to adapt quickly to sudden changes also helps actors in the long run because we learn to juggle and adjust at a rapid pace. That goes a long way with directors. They remember that.

I really like the way our working schedule is set up. Every sitcom has its own work calendar, but I think ours is hard to beat. We usually have a four-day workweek. One week a month we work five days—so for that particular week, we work on Monday. And the week that we work five days is always the week after we've had a one-week hiatus. A hiatus is a break or a short time off. This can be anywhere from a week to several months. When our show "goes down" at the end of the production season, we usually have four and one-half months off between seasons.

On the week each month that I'm on hiatus, I go to regular school. I walk the halls, change classes, and eat in the school cafeteria with all the other kids. I'm just another student. During the other weeks, I go to school on the set of *Step*.

Let's take a week in which I work a full five days, and I'll show you what a typical week is like, okay?

My Schedule

I get up at 7:00 A.M., and my mom and I leave for the studio at 7:30. I don't eat breakfast at home because cast members usually eat on the set. The production company provides a breakfast of bagels, cereal, pancakes, or eggs.

We begin with a table reading. This is where the entire cast, producers, writers, and director all sit around a big table and read through the script out loud. It's a closed reading—that means no visitors are allowed. Parents, guardians, and the guest cast are also in this room, but no one outside this circle of people can be there.

This is the first time we've read the script together. It's also considered a "rough" script. In other words, we know there will be changes made. For instance, it might be too long or too short, and dialogue will either be added or deleted. The script for each episode has to be an exact twenty-one minutes and thirty-seven seconds. The rest of the thirty-minute time slot is filled with commercials. So while we're reading through the script for the first time, the script supervisor is carefully timing the process.

Even though this is a cold reading, we still read it as though we're acting it out. We work on voice inflection, volume, and even facial expression. If the script isn't as funny as the producers and writers want it to be, they begin making changes that very day.

After our table reading, I either go to wardrobe for fitting, or I go on to class. I don't have to go to wardrobe every week because I usually wear normal clothes. Let me explain.

▼ ▼ ▼ ▼ ▼

People think I get a lot of attention, but I really don't. I'm not the most popular kid on the set.

At the beginning of each season, the wardrobe personnel will purchase clothes for each cast member to wear throughout the season and from time to time will add to our closets. Unless we're in a big growing spurt (which can easily happen to kid actors), we can usually wear most of what we've received throughout the season.

Once in a while, a cast member will need a special outfit. For example, if someone is going to have to dress up as a bird, he or she will need a special wardrobe fitting. When I dressed punk for the 1994 Halloween special, I had to have a special fitting. Most of the time, an actor only needs extra fittings with the wardrobe department when he or she has to wear something special or unusual. The exception is the guest cast. They always need to be fitted because obviously, they don't have a closet of clothes the company has provided for them.

School on the Set

So we're off to class. I go to school with Christine Lakin (she plays Al Lambert) and Josh Byrne (he plays Brendon Lambert). The other cast members are all over eighteen years of age. Our school is actually a trailer right outside the set. It has two rooms in it. One room has a computer (which is really old) and bean bags to sit on. This room is used for special study. The other room is a basic classroom with private desks.

We have a terrific teacher. Miss Salerno is Italian and in her early thirties. She's a lot of fun, and she makes learning a real adventure. She loves turtles and keeps a few as pets in our classroom. She even has her own special turtle language that she talks to them with. It's hilarious! She calls them torts and treats them as if they were people.

Miss Salerno is also really big on holidays. We have a little tree in the class that she decorates for each special occasion. Obviously, for Christmas, it was a Christmas tree. For Easter, it was an Easter tree, for Thanksgiving, a Thanksgiving tree, etc. Like I said, she really makes being in her class a lot of fun.

But aside from the good times, we also have a lot of work. We're not just sitting in desks pretending that we're working. The government is pretty strict about how many hours actors under the age of eighteen have to actually be in school. The very *minimum* amount of time I can be in school in one sitting is twenty minutes. I complete approximately sixteen hours of school in one week. We're juggling several different subjects (just like regular school), and we cram for tests and beg for no homework.

▼ ▼ ▼ ▼ ▼

> **I complete approximately sixteen hours of school in one week. We're juggling several different subjects (just like regular school), and we cram for tests and beg for no homework.**

It can get hectic. For instance, I might be right in the middle of a geometry equation and get called to the set for thirty minutes. If I've been in class for at least twenty minutes, I can go. If not, I have to complete my twenty minutes first. After my part is over, I immediately go right back to my desk and try to jump back into geometry again. I remain in class until I'm called back on the set.

I take an hour lunch break around 1:00 P.M. I usually just eat right there on the set with my mom. Again, the production company provides food, and we usually have a choice of soup or sandwiches. Once in a while I'll bring my lunch or leave the studio and eat somewhere close by. The times I leave are usually when I'm meeting a reporter for an interview or meeting with my publicist.

Many times I eat at the commissary (it's like a nice-looking cafeteria and is located on the lot). Sometimes I see actors from other TV shows or from films that are being shot on the Warner Brothers lot. Who and what you see can get pretty interesting! For instance, a group of actors might walk in with fake blood all over them because they've just shot a hospital scene. On one of our *Step by Step* episodes, many of the actors' parents were used as extras to fill up a crowd scene. Since this particular show depicted an earlier era, they all walked into the commissary wearing 1940s clothing. It can be pretty funny at times!

After lunch we work on blocking: where I will stand and walk, what I'll do physically, and what I'll hold in my hand. Nothing is ever done without rehearsing it first. When you see me casually walk across the kitchen, open the fridge, and pour myself a glass of orange juice, it's been rehearsed. When J.T. comes in and plops down on the sofa, he's rehearsed it. Each actor learns exactly where he's supposed to go and what he's expected to do. We also work on our lines . . . even though we know they'll probably be rewritten.

I'm in school for most of the rest of the day, and we finally leave the studio around 6:00 P.M. We usually have homework, and I try to get most of mine done on the way home. And since L.A. is known for its horrendous rush-hour traffic, I always have a lot of time to work with.

All Over Again?

On Tuesday I get up at the same time, and I leave the house again at 7:30 A.M. I arrive at the studio, grab a bite to eat for breakfast, get a script (we receive a new script every day with additional changes), and go straight to class. Depending on whether I'm heavy or light in the script determines when I'm called to the set. If I'm heavy (a lot of lines), I'm called between 9:00 and 9:30 A.M. If I'm light (only a few lines), I can stay in class, get more schoolwork done, and receive a later call.

Because *Step by Step* has a large cast, not everyone can be the center of attention every week. Sometimes I have several lines and the entire show revolves around me. Other times I may have only one or two lines.

I try to think of all this as a recipe. When you bake a cake you need flour, sugar, and a bunch of other ingredients. Sometimes I'm just a teaspoon of vanilla, and everyone else is a tablespoon of sugar. But you always need the teaspoon to complement the tablespoon. Sometimes I'm just a setup (one- or two-liners) for the bigger jokes. It's okay. Every ingredient—and every line—is important to the product as a whole.

▼ ▼ ▼ ▼ ▼

Sometimes I'm just a teaspoon of vanilla, and everyone else is a tablespoon of sugar. But you always need the teaspoon to complement the tablespoon.

After lunch, I either go back to class or back to rehearsal. At 4:00 P.M. we do a run-through for the producers. The writers are also there, and we're being watched on our staging. If something seems uncomfortable (like it might be too awkward for someone to jump over the couch and grab the TV remote with the timing that the script calls for), it usually gets changed.

As soon as we're finished with one scene, the producers and director discuss what they liked and didn't like. The writers then make changes in the script. After we've completed an entire run-through (we've finished the whole script), we all sit in the living room and discuss the additions or deletions. We compare notes and make sure we've all written down the same changes. We've also been timed, so by now we have a pretty accurate idea of how close we are to that twenty-one minutes and thirty-seven seconds goal.

Sometimes it can feel like a long day. I've often put in nine and one-half hours by the time I leave for home.

And Again?

Wednesday is pretty much the same, only this time we do a network *and* a producer run-through. On Thursday we do camera blocking. And on Friday it's show time!

I don't have to arrive until 12:45 P.M. on Fridays. I go straight to class for one hour with no interruptions. After that we have a dress run-through. That means each actor dresses exactly how he or she will appear for the actual taping. For instance, if I'm supposed to be dressed up like a dog, I'll wear the costume during this rehearsal.

Then it's time for the taping.

This Is for Real!

We actually begin taping the show at 6:00 P.M. on Friday evenings. We're located on the Warner Brothers lot in Stage Eight. We can fit about two hundred people into the studio audience. The tickets are free.

Many people are from out of town and have always wanted to see a TV taping. We also have several locals— people who live in Southern California, but just want something unique to do for the evening. It really is a lot of fun and the chairs always seem packed.

A professional comedian warms up the audience and also explains the taping process. He answers questions and gives away a lot of cool stuff during the evening. Since every scene is usually taped twice (sometimes to get a different camera angle, and other times because of a goof), the comedian's job is to keep the audience entertained during the in-between times. Every time a scene is reshot, the crew has to set up again. For instance, if we're eating dinner, before we can tape the scene again, it has to be set up exactly the same way we started the first time. That might mean more food is brought in or glasses refilled. It's important that we get all the details perfect.

Several TV monitors hang in front of the studio audience, so they can either watch the action on the floor, or they can see a closer view from the monitor.

The comedian often asks people where they're from and gives away autographed photos of the cast members. During the course of the evening, he'll give away *Step by Step* hats, T-shirts, and even a Suzanne Somers Thigh-Master.

Gettin' the Goods

But it's not always easy to grab one of these souvenirs. Often the comedian will "work" the people in the audience. For example, to win the Thigh-Master, you have to create a song with the word "thigh-master" somewhere in it and be willing to sing it in front of the entire studio audience!

▼ ▼ ▼ ▼ ▼

**To win the Thigh-Master, you have
to create a song with the word
"thigh-master" somewhere in it!**

Sometimes, while a room is being set up, we can hear the songs. And they're a total riot. Some are just stupid, others are really funny, and some are really pretty good. After each person sings his creation, the audience decides who the winner is by clapping the loudest for their specific choice. That person then receives the coveted Thigh-Master.

Direction

We don't have one particular director who coordinates our action for the entire season. We use several different directors, and I think that's good because it makes us better actors. Just like a football coach, each director has his own way of doing things. The more people we work with, the more variety we have in doing things.

Each director uses different techniques. Some are faster than others. Some use more close-ups; others use a greater variety of camera angles. Each director comes to the set with his or her own credentials and experience that makes him or her good. One of our directors, Richard Correll, used to be on the *Leave It to Beaver* show. He played Beaver's childhood friend Richard. Next time you're watching it on reruns, look for him!

Because each scene is usually taped at least twice, we finish somewhere between 8:30 to 10:00 P.M. At the close of the taping, the entire cast comes out front for a curtain call. We all take our bows and head back to our dressing rooms. We leave our clothes in the dressing room closet (remember, they belong to the studio, not us), and head home . . . unless someone from the audience has permission to come backstage and meet us.

If a visitor has permission, he wears a special wristband. That tag will alert guards that he has approval to walk around on the set after the show. To get a wristband, a guest has to have special permission from a cast member or someone working with the cast (like a publicist or camera person). They aren't handed out casually. We have to be very careful about letting strangers backstage.

After an exhausting day preparing and taping, I usually fall asleep in the car during the one and one-half hours it takes to get home.

Steps to a Good Theme

One of the things I appreciate most about *Step by Step* is the fact that our show always has some kind of message. In other words, we're not simply entertaining for entertainment's sake. There's usually a lesson, something positive to think about, by the end of the show.

▼ ▼ ▼ ▼ ▼

**One of the things I appreciate most
about Step by Step is the fact that
our show always has some kind
of message.**

It's never hammered or forced; the audience doesn't feel like we're pointing a big finger in their faces, but in a subtle way we're getting across some good ideas. One show dealt with J.T.'s low grades. He was tired of being made fun of, and Cody assumed he simply wasn't trying hard enough.

By the end of the show, though, it was discovered that J.T. had dyslexia, a learning disability that hinders reading. A person with dyslexia may see the letters in a word backward or reversed. Several thousand people suffer from this learning disability, and our show offered hope by challenging those who have dyslexia to do something about it. Once a person learns how to deal with dyslexia, he or she can lead a normal life and achieve as much as anyone else, as we showed in the program.

Another time we dealt with suicide. One of Cody's friends came to visit, and they boarded a small plane for skydiving. Once airborne, though, his friend unhooked his parachute and planned to jump out of the plane and kill himself. By talking with him, Cody learned that his friend's wife had died, and he couldn't cope with the loss. The show dealt with learning how to handle your problems instead of running away from them.

Another episode showed J.T. and Al driving the family vehicle when they had specifically been told not to drive. Al wrecked the truck, and they lied and tried to fix the damage themselves. Eventually they were found out, and our viewers were reminded of the importance of listening to and obeying parents.

And Then There's Sex

More than once, *Step by Step* has dealt with sexuality. We aired an episode a few years ago in which Cody and J.T. met a couple of good-looking girls who wanted to take them back to their apartment. J.T. reacted like many teen guys would and was jumping at the chance.

Cody, however, turned down the proposition. Of course, J.T. gave him a hard time about his decision, boasting that this was the opportunity of a lifetime. Cody simply explained to his cousin that he was a virgin—and not by accident. Cody had consciously chosen to remain celebate until marriage because he didn't want to cheat his future wife. What a positive message, huh? And believe it or not, we received more mail from that particular episode than any other show we've done to date. People of all ages wrote letters saying, "On most TV shows you hear about people having sex. Thanks for being different and taking a stand."

▼ ▼ ▼ ▼ ▼

If someone's making fun of you, try this on them: "You must really feel bad about yourself to make fun of me. 'Cause if you felt good, you'd try to make others feel good too."

In another episode regarding sex, Cody had been invited to join a fraternity on his college campus. They were hosting a huge party one night, and Cody invited Karen to go. Dana had warned her that a fraternity party probably wouldn't be the place she'd want to end up on a Friday night, but she went anyway.

When Cody left the room, one of the guys began making sexual advances toward Karen. He asked her to accompany him upstairs to his bedroom. When she refused, he continued to pressure her until finally saying, "What's wrong? Are you a virgin or something?"

When Karen didn't respond, he knew he had guessed right. He influenced the other frat guys to join him in making fun of her. Cody reentered the room, and seeing what was happening, approached the fraternity president and grabbed him by his shirt collar.

"So what if she's a virgin?" he said. "I'm a virgin, too, and I think that's pretty cool. You got a problem with that?" He then took Karen's hand, drove her home, and dropped out of the fraternity. And one by one, all the other girls at the party left because they, too, wanted to be respected and treated like women instead of like sex objects. Without preaching, we were able to promote what I believe is an extremely valuable message about abstinence.

The Night I Went Wild

For our 1994 Halloween episode, our writers completely changed my character. Normally I play the role of a conservative, intellectual kid. For this particular show, however, I was influenced by a girl who was really wild.

Because I wanted to be liked and admired by her, I did several things Mark usually wouldn't do. He threw his values and standards aside just to be attractive to this girl.

My behavior wasn't the only thing that changed. I even dressed completely different. The makeup and wardrobe department applied a fake tattoo; I wore black jeans with huge holes ripped in the knees and a red bandanna around my right thigh.

I sported spiked leather collars around my neck and wrist, and a sleeveless black leather jacket. My hair was *really* wild! Our makeup artist first applied a skull cap to my head (it fits over your real hair and makes you look bald), then attached a wig. It was a five-inch spike that stood straight up! At the base of my hairline it was white but it slowly blended into a pink then a bright fuschia on top. It was really funny!

The girl I was with convinced me to egg houses with her, and we ended up getting caught. As the police patrolled the neighborhood, they saw what we were doing and took us down to the police station.

In an enjoyable way, we were able to tell kids that it's not worth it to toss your values aside just to be liked and accepted by someone. It was a fun show.

Fatal Addiction?

Another episode centered around my becoming addicted to video games. Frank wanted to help me loosen up from obsessing over my schoolwork and grades, so he purchased a video game set and installed it onto the television. As the show progressed, I switched my obsession with grades to an obsession with the video game set. Nothing else seemed important anymore. I let everything else go, including my personal hygiene.

They finally enrolled me in group therapy for video game addicts. It was a humorous show that taught a powerful message: It's important to keep everything in perspective. Grades are important, but so is a well-rounded lifestyle. When we obsess over *anything,* we need to take a second look at our priorities.

To make a positive point in a fun and entertaining way is really quite a challenge for a twenty-one minute, thirty-seven second sitcom. That's why I appreciate the fact that *Step* goes the extra mile in striving for excellence.

Back to the Big Screen!

After our third season of *Step by Step,* I was offered the recurring role of Ted Newton in *Beethoven's 2nd.* I was ecstatic! It was great to be with the cast again, and I was especially looking forward to working with all the puppies.

Beethoven's 2nd took a little longer to film than *Beethoven.* We worked on the first movie for five months and the second for seven months. The reason it took longer was because we had to increase the number of dogs used. And unlike most humans, St. Bernards grow at an incredibly fast pace in a very short time. Think of it this way: Out of all the people in the cast, no one had to replace their wardrobe in the seven months it took us to film. If we had been fitting the dogs for wardrobe, though, we would've constantly been switching clothes for them.

Another reason the sequel took longer than the original movie was because there were so many animals being used, and we had more retakes to complete. Even the most well-trained animals can be stubborn, confused, or sick. It takes a lot of patience to work with them.

▼ ▼ ▼ ▼ ▼

Most of the time, working with the animals was almost like working with professional people.

Fortunately, Beethoven and his friends had one of the best trainers in the nation. Most of the time, working with the animals was almost like working with professional people. They were always friendly. They didn't bite or attack. These dogs were wonderful! And, yeah, we three kids *loved* playing with them!

A Special Surprise

My thirteenth birthday rolled around while I was involved with *Beethoven's 2nd*. We were filming in Montana, and I was pretty bummed that I couldn't have a party or be at home for my birthday. During lunchtime, the production company (with the help of the caterer) surprised me with a big cake. It had a forest on it because we were doing a forest scene.

Then later that night, my family, a few friends, and my on-location teacher, Gloria, surprised me with another party and gave me golf gifts at our condo. It was really fun. Everyone sang "Happy Birthday," and it really took the sting out of being away on my thirteenth birthday.

Rollin' Out the Red Carpet

Every motion picture has a "screening." That's when it's showed as a special preview to the cast and selected guests. It's really fun. At the screening of *Beethoven's 2nd,* my whole family (the real one) was picked up in a stretch limousine outside our home. The limo was really cool! It was black and looked like a fresh wax job had just been done on it. The seats were leather, and there was a TV, stereo, telephone, and refreshment center loaded with soft drinks. It was incredible!

The driver took us to the City Walk outside of Universal Studios. City Walk is a wild, crazy, super-fun shopping mall that's always crowded. The Cineplex Theater is located there, and that's where the screening was being held. Our driver opened our doors, and we stepped out onto a big piece of red carpet that led from our limo to the theater entrance. It was around Christmastime, so the whole place just seemed alive with excitement!

Right outside the doors of the theater were some huge wooden doghouses. One had "Beethoven" painted on it, and another one had "Missy" on the front. The other doghouses were for all the puppies in the movie.

On the other side of the red carpet were huge cardboard cutouts of the Newton family with the dogs. It was amazing how lifelike they looked!

The teen magazine reporters were there, along with all the paparazzi. All the refreshments were complimentary, so we filled up on popcorn and soft drinks.

Every actor always enjoys seeing his name flash across the screen during credits, and this is especially exciting at a screening, because it's the first time he or she has seen it. In the first *Beethoven* movie, the names of the three of us who played the Newton children all appeared together on screen—at the same time. But on *Beethoven's 2nd,* we each got to have our name appear individually. Now, this might not seem like a big deal to you, but it's really important to an actor.

All the producers and directors are at the screening, and the first time an actor appears on the screen, they all scream and yell for him or her. Imagine how excited I was to see my character appear on the screen for the first time and hear people in the audience yelling, "Hey, Chris! All right!" It's a lot of fun.

▼ ▼ ▼ ▼ ▼

Imagine how excited I was to see my character appear on screen for the first time and hear people in the audience yelling, "Hey, Chris!"

Another thing that makes a screening so exciting is that this is also the first time we get to hear any of the music. It's really cool to see how it all fits together and enhances a frightening or tense moment.

In any movie, more footage is shot than is actually used, and of course, we never know for sure what will be used and what won't. So we're sitting there thinking, *Hey, they never used such and such* or *I thought they'd end up taking that out, but they didn't.*

The whole experience is a lot of fun and creates a special memory for each member of the cast and crew.

It's Not Always What It Seems

When it comes to Hollywood, don't believe everything you read. So much is written in the tabloids, and so much gossip floats around that I know it's difficult for the general public to know what's really true.

I've been fortunate. I haven't been in the tabloids very much. Some actors are constantly being written about. I guess I'm lucky.

My Tabloid Exposure

My first tabloid experience was an article that said the *Full House* kids and the three youngest *Step by Step* kids didn't get along. It said how much we hated each other and were always fighting. Not only that, but it had gotten so bad, the *Full House* kids were finally banned from coming around the *Step* set.

False. Every word of it. First of all, not only do we get along, but we actually enjoy each other's company quite a bit. We don't get to see a lot of each other, but since both shows were filmed on the Warner Brothers property, we did bump into each other occasionally.

Friday nights are tape nights for all the T.G.I.F. shows except for *Boy Meets World*. They tape on the Disney lot on a different night. Anyway, *Full House* and *Step by Step* had dinner together every week. The *Step* cast usually goes in for dinner between 4:00 to 5:30 P.M. The *Full House* cast usually arrived right before us. It was a fun time of unwinding before taping that night's show, and it's neat just to chat with other teen actors outside of our own show.

▼ ▼ ▼ ▼ ▼

**Every actor I know hates being in
the tabloids. I guess that's because
almost everything that's printed
about them is false.**

The second time I appeared in a tabloid was because of our Halloween show. The tabloid was covering several TV sitcoms and showing what each was doing for their Halloween special, and because this particular episode of *Step* centered around me, I was highlighted.

Every actor I know hates being in the tabloids. I guess that's because almost everything that's printed about them is false. Those kinds of papers make their money out of sensationalizing negative rumors. At least the second time I was in *The National Enquirer* it wasn't gossip—just plain coverage about our show.

The Public Never Knows

I've already let you in on some "secrets" of the entertainment biz, but there are other things that go on with taping a weekly show that the audience probably never thinks about.

For instance, sometimes we get sick. And unlike most other jobs—where you can simply call in ill—"the show must go on." I remember one time I had pulled a muscle playing basketball, but on Friday night when we were ready to tape, I was there and was determined to act normal.

Another time I had a virus and was running a low fever. Even though physically it would have felt great to stay in bed, my heart was with the show. I showed up on tape night and acted as though I was well. And it's not just me; every actor does this. That's what being a professional is all about. And that's what *acting* is all about—acting like you feel great when you're really achy and weak all over.

Another time I had a bad cold and had been hoarse all week. My doctor gave me some antibiotics and cough medicine to help clear up the congestion in my throat. Minutes before the show started, I was backstage using nasal and throat spray and gargling so I wouldn't sound like I was sick. When the show starts to roll and you're sick, the goal is not to sound like you have a cold. The goal is to appear normal.

What You See Is What You Get

Occasionally the script calls for me to do or say something that goes against my personal values. There's no such thing as a perfect script. Often there's something in an actor's dialogue that he'd rather change or say a different way.

I'm fortunate to get to work with producers and directors who have been extremely understanding when I've felt uncomfortable with a specific portion of the script. For instance, I've never had to take God's name in vain. I'm extremely uncomfortable with that. It's been in the script before, but after explaining my convictions to the producers, I've gotten it changed.

Some actors aren't so fortunate. They may work for someone who says, "We hired you to follow the script, and you signed a contract. Do it our way."

Other actors simply don't care about cursing. It's not a

big deal to them, therefore, they don't fight it. I want to be a positive role model, though. And I'd feel hypocritical using language on the screen that I don't even use in real life.

These are things the audience never knows about, though. Most people assume that what's said and done on the show has simply been memorized from a script. They're not aware of the fact that sometimes actors are saying what they're saying because they've taken a stand against an earlier script and have asked for a change.

Selective But Not Picky

I also know my limits. Just because I work for some terrific people doesn't mean I can whine and ask for a change in dialogue every time I don't like what's being said. That's being picky. The only time I ask for a change is when the script calls for me to do something that's in conflict with my personal beliefs. That's simply being selective.

If you read chapter 15, you'll discover my decision to remain sexually pure until marriage. In light of that decision, I don't want to play a character who's sexually involved outside of marriage. So I choose my battles carefully, and most of the time I'm respected for taking a stand.

▼ ▼ ▼ ▼ ▼

You don't know about the battle I may have already fought—before the show was taped—to change lines that were even harder to say.

You may be disappointed with something I say sometime on a show. But remember, all you're seeing is what's being filmed on the screen in front of you. You don't know about the battle I may have already fought—before the show was taped—to change lines that were even harder to say. Again, I have to be selective, and I have to choose my battles carefully.

In Front of the Camera

Often you'll see a crowd scene in a show. It looks like the cameraman simply went outside and filmed people walking across the street, or people sitting in the stands at a basketball game. What you may not realize is that every one of the people you see on screen has been selected to be there.

These people are often referred to as "extras." Their job is to make up the "atmosphere" of a particular scene. For instance, if the camera is focusing on two cast members at a table in a restaurant, you'll notice people behind them at other tables. This creates the desired atmosphere the director is striving for.

My sister, Bethany, was even an extra in the *Step by Step* 1994 Halloween episode. She and several other children were dressed in various costumes and were shown in the background collecting candy from door to door. (This created a realistic mood of being in a neighborhood filled with children.) She was dressed in a pink fairy-princess costume. She loved it! My mom has also been an extra on *Step.* Extras are usually paid between $50 to $100 per day for simply being in the background.

So even though it might *look* as though the people in the background were caught on film by chance, remember that nothing happens by accident. Each scene is carefully planned and rehearsed. Hollywood is full of surprises . . . and that's one of the things that makes acting so fun!

Between Steps

My mom is always on the set with me. Know why? According to the law, anyone who's under the age of eighteen is considered a minor and has to have a guardian on the set at all times until he or she is sixteen years old.

Some actors choose to hire a manager to do this. When I started acting, my parents decided that instead of paying someone outside the family to watch me, my mom would assume that role. She and Dad feel that if I act up (hey, I'm a teen! I'm *not* perfect), she should be the one who disciplines me. I think they're also concerned that if someone outside the family was watching me instead of my parents, that person may choose to let some of my actions go unnoticed or unpunished.

You gotta understand that I'm a good kid; I really am. But my parents are pretty strict. And I know it's for my own good . . . because that's what they constantly tell me. So every now and then when I am out of line, Mom deals with it immediately. And you know what? I really would rather have someone from my own family making me toe the line instead of someone who's simply doing it for money.

▼　▼　▼　▼　▼

**Once you start treating your parents
with respect—real respect—you'll be
amazed at what you can learn
from them!**

Mom's Job

Just because she's on the set with me every day doesn't mean she's watching me like a hawk. She spends a lot of time in my dressing room reading and taking care of business.

Since she's acting as my manager, it's up to her to decide which things I should and shouldn't do. For instance, I'm involved in several charities. I obviously can't do everything, but after we discuss them, Mom selects those that she knows I'll enjoy. She also helps arrange my airline schedule and generally keeps all the loose ends tied together.

Work *and* Play

I don't like a lot of free time. I get bored just sitting around, so I really enjoy being involved in various charities. It's work, but it's also a lot of fun! It makes me feel good to be able to help others.

One of the most exciting charities I joined was the Juvenile Diabetes Foundation. They hosted an eight-day celebrity cruise. Several diabetic children were on the ship along with teen actors. It was work, but it was *enjoyable* work.

I played a lot of Ping-Pong with the children and helped with the games and relays. In one particular race, the goal was to see which team could wrap up the celebrity the fastest. The kids wrapped me up in toilet paper. I looked like a mummy. After I was totally covered with paper, they had to decorate me. It was a blast, and we got second place.

Some of the other actors on the cruise with me were Ryder Strong (Shaun on *Boy Meets World*), Andrea Barber (Kimmy on *Full House*), Jenna Von Oy (Six on *Blossom*), Danielle Fishel (Topanga on *Boy Meets World*), and Tia and Tamara Mowry (twins on *Sister, Sister*).

Ryder and I knew each other from work we had done together—we both landed a guest appearance on *Going Places* a few years ago in which we were dressed as Cub Scouts. Ryder's a terrific guy, and we share some things in common. Besides having the same agent, we both love basketball, and since we're both on ABC sitcoms, we usually run into each other at network parties.

Tia, Tamara, and I all found out (during this particular week) that we also had something in common. Both of our parents wouldn't let us stay out past 1:00 A.M. And that was just during the cruise. At home, I'd never get to stay out that late!

Our parents have some of the same rules and guidelines. Their parents and my parents wanted to make sure that we understood our 1:00 A.M. curfew was something special and not to be repeated. I remember Dad saying, "A cruise is a self-contained environment. It's not like you can leave the ship! So your mom and I are allowing you to stay out much later than usual. But don't start thinking you'll get to do this at home!" Tia and Tamara's parents said the same thing.

The twins are great girls! And, yeah, they really *do* talk at the same time and say the same things. They're a blast to be around!

It's Not All Fun and Games

I'm also very involved in charities that work with kids who have serious, even fatal diseases. The Children's Wish Foundation is an organization that grants wishes to children with fatal afflictions. The Ronald McDonald House is also involved with terminally ill young people.

I appreciate the opportunity to be able to touch their lives—even in a small way. I often go to the hospitals and just sit on the edge of the bed and talk with them. Sometimes they'll have a Nintendo set up, and we'll play a few games together.

I am always amazed at the courage these kids have. I saw one girl who had bone marrow cancer, lying in bed with a "cage" around her leg. She had pins in her leg and it was literally encased in a circle of metal to keep the pins from being knocked or bumped. She was only nine years old, yet she had such a terrific attitude.

Sometimes I'll get to hold the babies and walk around the room with them. Some of these kids have been abused, and many have serious illnesses, but most are terminally ill. They know they're going to die, and they still have the courage to smile and try to have a positive outlook.

▼ ▼ ▼ ▼ ▼

I cherish my involvement in these kinds of charities. Know why? Because it helps me not take life for granted.

I cherish my involvement in these kinds of charities. Know why? Because it helps me not take life for granted. It reminds me how *valuable* life is! I mean, think about it . . . every time we even take a breath, it's a gift. I don't want to get used to being in good health; I want to always appreciate it.

Sometimes, if I can't get something I want or I have a rotten day, I think about the babies I've held or the kids I've visited who only have a limited time to live, and it rearranges my priorities real fast.

I wish I could offer these patients a cure or give them a batch of hope. Usually the most I can do is simply show them I care by taking the time to be with them. And I hope that by giving up my Saturdays or vacation time, I can somehow make a small difference in their lives.

Just Ordinary People?

Andrea Barber and I do a lot of the same charity events. We sat next to each other recently while signing autographs at a Ronald McDonald House for children who have cancer. On *Full House* she plays the dippy neighbor, but in real life she's very grounded. The thing we share in common is that both of our parents go out of their way to keep us normal.

Being in front of the cameras all the time and sometimes getting special treatment can cause one to start thinking he *deserves* attention. My parents and Andrea's parents do a great job of making sure we don't forget that it's a *privilege* to act instead of taking it for granted.

Andrea and I got to be pretty good friends on the cruise, and we both feel the same way about our careers: We don't want to be placed on a pedestal simply because we happen to have a job that's noticed by the public. We're just normal kids who happen to be acting at this time in our lives.

I'm grateful for the opportunities to be involved in a variety of charities between tapings of *Step by Step*. It widens my circle of friends and increases my knowledge about different things.

Happy Birthday to me! Mr. Outgoing on my third birthday.

Here I am in kindergarten, sporting the eye patch that other kids made fun of.

Even at an early age, I loved dressing up and pretending to be different people.

My first paycheck! I got this after the McDonald's commercial.

"Four score and seven years ago . . ." I always wanted to be the president of the United States.

Captain Chris. We had the coolest pirate ship at the park. You can imagine how often I went there.

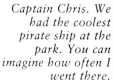

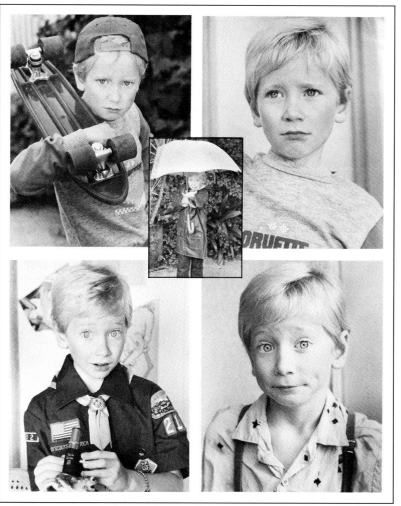

My first composite. The casting people wanted to see different looks. What do you think?

I absolutely love flying and hope to someday have a pilot's license.

My family and me on the Juvenile Diabetes Foundation cruise. Left to right: Bethany, Mom (Donna), me, and Dad (Jon).

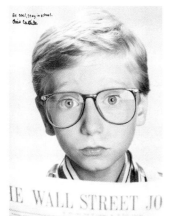

Be cool, stay in school.
Chris Castile

This is the first fan mail postcard I sent out to fans when they wrote in. I was eleven.

This is my current headshot for auditions. Big difference, isn't it?

Beethoven's first bath in the original movie. From left to right: Nicholle Tom, Beethoven, me, and Sara Rose Karr. © *Universal City Studios, Inc.*

Okay, I'll probably never have a Porsche, let alone a Porsche limo. But I can pretend, can't I?

It's always nice to take a break between scenes!

My Step by Step *family:* (standing) Staci Keanan, Patrick Duffy, Suzanne Somers, Angela Watson, Brandon Call, Sasha Mitchell, (seated) Josh Byrne, Christine Lakin, and me. © Warner Bros.

It was great getting to work with my sister, Bethany, during the Halloween episode. Don't you just love the hair?

I love my mom, and I'm not afraid to show it!

"And . . . action!" On location during Beethoven's 2nd.

Me with Rosetta LeNoire (Grandma Winslow on Family Matters.) She and I are pals.

Me with my Beethoven's 2nd *family. Left to right: Missy, Sara Rose Karr, Nicholle Tom, Beethoven, Bonnie Hunt, Charles Grodin, and me with the puppies.* © *Universal City Studios, Inc.*

Step by Step *director Rich Correll is totally into Halloween, so he was perfect to direct the Halloween episode.*

It looks like the real thing, but it's actually Mom and me with a stuffed Beethoven.

Travels within the Circuit

I've had the privilege of doing a variety of appearances and activities outside the series, and I really enjoy it. They're fun, and I enjoy the experience I gain from them. I get to meet a wide variety of people.

Golf, of Course

I'm a golf nut. I really am. I love all sports, but I've been playing golf for about seven years now, and it is my very favorite. I can hit 220 yards off the tee, and I shoot in the high 70s on a good day. My best score ever is a 74. Since I live in Southern California, I can play golf year round. I usually play about twice a month.

One of my most memorable events was getting to play in Michael Jordan's celebrity golf tournament. I didn't actually get to play *with* him, but I got to play some other incredible athletes.

To date, I'm the youngest person ever invited to play in the Greater Greensboro Pro-Am tournament in its twenty-eight-year history. I feel honored that I got to play with so many adult celebrities.

My favorite golfer of all time is Greg Garmon. I ordered some golf clubs just like his, and I had them set to my own specifications for height, shaft, and grip.

Since I'm so crazy about the sport, I try to keep up with the stats. Male professional golfers who are in the top fifty can make approximately $150,000 a year. It's not as high for the female pros, but they have a lot of cool tournaments in fun places.

A Special Memory

A couple of years ago, I was invited to board an aircraft carrier, and because of my love for planes, I was ecstatic! We got to make a hook landing. That means you make a 60-degree turn toward the aircraft carrier. As you're approaching the carrier, a hook comes down from the aircraft and attaches to one of the resting wires . . . if you're lucky. We missed the first two times, but actually hooked on our third try. When the hook is successful, the aircraft stops abruptly on the carrier.

▼　▼　▼　▼　▼

**A couple of years ago, I was invited
to board an aircraft carrier, and
because of my love for planes,
I was ecstatic!**

This was a cargo plane for the Navy, and all the seats were built backwards. The pilot sits forward, of course, but everyone else sits backward. It's really cool! They open up the back of the plane, and you can parachute out. This particular aircraft was a twenty-seater and was also used for parachuting.

We flew three hundred miles from San Diego to the *Carl Vincent, Number 70*. After arriving, I signed autographs and toured the aircraft. They made me an honorary chief. I got to eat with the chief. We had pizza and steak. It was fun but hard, because I had to live like a Navy person. I stayed through the night and the day after. It was quite a memorable experience!

The Talk Show Circuit

One thing's for certain: Talk shows are never dull! The exciting thing about being a guest is that you never know for sure what's going to happen. Oh, you're told ahead of time what you'll be talking about, and sometimes you're even prepped (given a list of questions before the show), but the element of surprise is always there.

Some of the talk shows I've done are: *Good Morning, America; Inside Edition; E: Entertainment; The Mike and Maty Show; The Marilu Show; The Vicki Show; The Suzanne Somers Show; KTLA Morning Show* (Southern California); and *The Dini Petty Show* (Canada).

▼ ▼ ▼ ▼ ▼

The exciting thing about being a guest is that you never know for sure what's going to happen.

I was also privileged to be a guest on *America's Funniest People* with Dave Coulier (who also plays Joey on *Full House*). Beethoven made a guest appearance with me, and we had a great time. Dave is just as fun and crazy in real life as he is on the show. Dave's just naturally funny. He's always on—never pretending. He impressed me as being extremely genuine. He also loves golf, so we got along great! I got to introduce some of the segments on the show, and I answered questions from the studio audience and from Dave.

On *Good Morning, America,* I got to introduce my *Beethoven* family. Guests are well taken care of on any talk show. They provided our flight, motel, food, all expenses during our stay, plus an honorarium for being on the show. A guest is paid approximately $1,000 to $1,500, depending on the show and the guest.

Surprise!

I really enjoyed doing *The Dini Petty Show* in Toronto. She and I chatted about golf for fifteen minutes before the show. She asked me how to correct her slice, and I tried to give her some quick tips. She's really a fun woman.

When I came onstage she started the conversation on golf and talked about how we had discussed it backstage. Then she asked me what my favorite candy was. When I said Skittles, she responded with, "Well, we know your birthday is coming up soon, and since you already have golf clubs, we decided not to get you more. But we do have some candy for you."

A stagehand walked onto the set and handed me a bubble gum machine *filled* with Skittles! It was a huge surprise. I hadn't suspected a thing. Dini had never eaten a Skittle before, and she asked me what they were. While I was explaining what they were, we kept trying to get the machine open, but I guess it was stuck.

Someone handed me a penny, so I put it in the slot, but the candy wouldn't come out. It was really funny! I asked if maybe it only took Canadian pennies, so she requested that the audience members look inside their wallets for pennies. They started throwing pennies at us! One hit me in the face and a few landed at my feet—they were all over the stage.

We kept trying to make it work, and finally Dini started banging on the top of it to try to get some of the Skittles out. I said, "I've got a screwdriver at home. I can just unscrew the top and pull them out by the handful."

She decided to change the subject and asked me about how I got into show business. Then she brought up the thing about my "President's suit." (Flip back to chapter 1 for a quick reminder.) So I recounted the times as a pre-schooler when I'd walk around the house giving "speeches" to Mom and Dad.

The other guests who were on the show the same day were model Beverly Johnson and singer Aaron Neville.

I'm Not Perfect

When I was on *The Vicki Show,* the entire episode revolved around teens and teen problems. We talked a lot about suicide and depression.

The audience was filled with teens. Several of them were dressed weird, and one kid even had blue hair. I was intimidated and thought they wouldn't like me because I seemed so straight compared to all of them. I didn't want to come off looking like I thought I was perfect, and I was really nervous about being asked questions by the studio audience.

▼   ▼   ▼   ▼   ▼

There are always consequences to telling a lie. Don't get into the habit.

As a result, I said some things to make the studio audience feel like I was one of them. I bragged about lying and getting in trouble. And though I have done that (what kid hasn't?), I exaggerated to try and impress them. I said something about getting clobbered. Well, I did get in trouble, but I wasn't actually "clobbered."

One of the guests was a psychologist, and he was really strange. He took the word "clobbered" and ran off on a tangent with it. He started talking about child abuse and kids who are beaten. That's not at all what I meant!

As the show progressed, and as I listened to different teens share their stories, I began to realize the difficult background many of them were from. It was then that I began to understand. *That's why he looks that way. He needs attention,* I thought. I learned an important lesson that day. I realized I can't judge someone just because he looks different from me. I have to try to get to know them from the *inside* out.

I was still pretty nervous by the end of the show, and I assumed the entire audience had probably written me off as a huge nerd. But as people were mingling and leaving, I overheard a pink-haired girl from the studio audience talking with a friend. She said, "That's the kid on *Step by Step*. I really like him."

Not only did her comment put me at ease, but it also taught me that I can't assume that I know what others are thinking. I need to think the best of others, and strive to believe that they're thinking the best about me.

If There's Time . . .

As my schedule allows, I also continue to do commercials. They provide a fun break from the weekly grind of a series, and I like the variety. You may have seen or heard me on any one of these: Capri Sun Fruit Drink, Mattel Bogglin, TJ Maxx, Kellogg's Honey Smacks, Vivid Detergent, Mattel HeMan, El Torrito Restaurant, Hunts Snack Pack Pudding, FAYGO Cola (a company located in Michigan), and Nintendo.

Between tapings of *Step by Step,* I also do a few T.G.I.F. spots each season. These are the promos that advertise each Friday night's lineup of shows. They're fun, but they're actually a lot tougher than they look. They have to be exactly twenty seconds. If it's over or under even one second, it can't be used.

The producers call me "One-Take Chris," because I usually get it done in exactly twenty seconds. I usually tape one T.G.I.F. promo every four shows. One time they put me in a dog house, and I delivered my lines from inside!

It Can't Be Done without ... Family!

I have a close-knit family, and I'm extremely grateful for them! There's a lot of stress in being a public person, and I gotta be honest: The glue that holds my life together is my family and my faith in God. Let's talk about my family first, okay?

My dad and mom (Jon and Donna) say it's important to find a lifemate who shares your same values. And I believe that values are important in a close-knit family.

Misconceptions

You may think that just because I'm on TV, I get to do what I want. *Wrong!* As I mentioned earlier, my parents are pretty strict with me. There are certain TV shows I'm not even allowed to watch. And I never get to see anything that's rated beyond PG-13. We usually only see PGs. Once in a while we'll take in a PG-13, but only after Mom and Dad have asked a lot of questions. (Good thing those *Beethoven* movies are PG, huh?)

▼　▼　▼　▼　▼

**You may think that just because I'm
on TV, I get to do what I want.
Wrong!**

Another misconception people often have is about my money. After all, actors make plenty of it, so we can buy whatever we want whenever we want, right? Wrong again!

I'll let you in on a little secret: I don't even know how much I make! That's right. Mom and Dad decided when I first started acting (remember those commercials I started with?) that they wouldn't tell me what salary I received because they didn't want me to get the big head.

So, no, I can't buy whatever I want. Most of my money is placed in a trust fund. I can't even get to it until I'm twenty-one! I do get an allowance, though—$20 a week— and that's only if I finish all my chores.

Some of my friends on the show purchased brand-new cars (really cool ones!) when they turned sixteen, but Mom and Dad have already laid down the law for me. "When you turn sixteen," they've said, "don't think we're going to take you out to purchase the most expensive or fancy car around. It's not going to happen. We *will* help you find a good, solid vehicle that will be reliable for the distance you have to drive to and from work."

Too Strict?

You may think that sounds a little too strict, but you know what? I kinda appreciate that. Oh, I wouldn't be honest if I didn't tell you there's nothing more I'd love to have than a fancy car! But deep inside . . . much deeper than what I want right now . . . is this appreciation for what they're teaching me.

See, I know that ultimately, cars will come and go. And instead of throwing my energy and my assets into something so temporary, I'll look back someday and be proud that I spent my time and money doing things that made a difference in people's lives.

Now don't go thinking I'm a saint. I'm not. And these lessons haven't been easy to learn. My parents and I go 'round and 'round sometimes about this kind of stuff. But the bottom line is that I'm thankful I have a mom and dad who care enough about who I turn out to be ten years from now, that they're making sure the difference starts showing up *now*.

Life on the Home Front

I've already mentioned that Mom is on the set with me during the day, and Dad is at work. My sister, Bethany, is eleven (she's four years younger than me). Other than Dougie, our longhaired dachshund, that's our entire family. We've lived in Southern California all my life, and even though we escaped the floods a few years back, we do have to deal with the occasional earthquakes.

We've lived in the same house for fifteen years, and yeah, part of my responsibilities include helping take care of that house. I have all kinds of chores to do. Probably some of the same ones you get stuck with. I have to get my room in order, take out the trash, clean the toilets, and help with the yard work.

▼ ▼ ▼ ▼ ▼

**I have all kinds of chores to do.
Probably some of the same ones
you get stuck with.**

What I absolutely hate, though, is picking up clothes and putting them in the hamper. We don't have hampers in our rooms—which is really lame . . . we used to, but now the hampers are in the garage. So we have to go all the way around to the garage (which is only thirty feet away, but when you're tired it feels like it takes forever to get there!), and we have to put them in color order.

We have five hampers, and they're all in a specific order. They're red, blue, green, black, and white. We do this so the red won't wash out on white, and so Mom won't have to throw them out. I know it's a lot easier for her, but it sure is a hassle sometimes.

My real mom sounds a little like my *Step by Step* mom, Carol, huh?

Growing Which Direction?

Often kids will try to pull away from their parents during the teen years . . . or give them the silent treatment . . . or do something that damages their relationship. Instead of getting away from my parents to "be myself," I've learned that they're the ones with whom I'm really free to be me! They know me better than anyone else in the world, so I'm taking advantage of that.

They're the ones with whom I'm sharing my insides. And they're also the people I run to when my world falls apart. See, they love me *completely*. I can be a total jerk around them and know that it won't decrease their love for me. (I may be grounded from TV for a week, but their love for me remains the same.) They help keep my feet on the ground, and help me to remain "real"—you know, "touchable." At the same time, though, they've instilled a genuine confidence within me. I guess what I'm really trying to say is, I get a lot of my security from them.

Show business can be a fleeting thing. A show can be canceled without much warning, actors can be written out of a show, or ratings can make an entire career nose-dive. If I based my security in what I'm doing, I'd be pretty insecure. My parents have taught me that my security must be settled in something that's *not* fleeting, something that *won't* change with the ratings. That *something* is my personal faith in God.

My parents consistently keep pointing me to God. And it's really my faith that pulls me through the bad days.

▼ ▼ ▼ ▼ ▼

**My parents consistently keep pointing
me to God. And it's really my faith
that pulls me through the bad days.**

Family Tightness

I realize that I'm pretty lucky to have the family I do. I know several kids my age who have horrible relationships with their parents. Well, like anything, a good relationship takes work and commitment. I'm committed to my family, and they're committed to me. To improve life on your home front, you also have to *care* about investing the time it'll take to make it happen. So for my friends reading this book who would like to make things better inside their homes, here's my advice. Since quality relationships are based on *CARE,* I've chosen to use that word to give you my suggestions, okay?

C: Concern

Make a conscious effort to show that you care. I try to demonstrate this to my mom and dad by doing a bunch of little things.

Since Mom's on the set with me all the time, I'll often grab something for her to eat and take it back to the dressing room so she won't have to go get it. Sometimes I run to the grocery store with her when I'd much rather stay at home. This shows her that I enjoy spending time together. And I try to remember to ask questions that will prompt good conversation, like "How was your day, Dad?" (See, you don't have to do something gigantic. If you do enough small stuff, eventually it all adds up to something much bigger!)

This takes a real mental effort, because I'm a self-centered guy. I have to really *think* about doing this. But concern is a two-way street. Mom and Dad make a conscious effort to show *me* they care, so it's sort of my duty to give back what they've given to me.

A: Answer

When your parents ask you how things are going, instead of giving them one-word answers, try complete sentences. Strive to realize that your parents really do care about what's going on in your life. And even though this may seem scary, the more they know, the more they can help!

This includes the big stuff too. If you're afraid of failing a class, or you're being pressured to join a gang, or you think you're pregnant, your folks need to know. If for some reason they don't do anything to help you, then tell another trusted adult.

▼ ▼ ▼ ▼ ▼

If things are rotten between your parents and you, make a date with them—a real date—and talk it out. Why? 'Cause there's too much at stake not to.

The goal? To make your parents your best friends. I realize I'm certainly in the minority when I say that, but I really believe it. See, I realize that twenty years from now the relationship I have with Mom and Dad is going to be an outcome of what I make of it right now! Someday when I'm married and have kids, I want to be able to turn to my folks as friends; that's why I'm trying to do all that's necessary to build a strong bond today.

R: Rituals

You might think this is corny, but I believe in traditions. Besides being important in creating family consistency, they're also just plain fun!

Does your family have some rituals—a few things that you do regularly? If not, try to create a few. Some of my favorite rituals in our family are really pretty simple things. For instance, we try to eat dinner together as often as possible. When I've had a rough day on the set, it sure feels good to come home and eat dinner with the family and to pray about problems I may have had during the day.

Because of our hectic schedule, Mom and Dad take turns cooking. That, too, is pretty fun! Dad makes some mean hot dogs, and he's even gotten pretty good at pizza. And Mom? Well, she can make *anything* taste good. She's terrific!

We also have a few Christmas rituals. We have a nativity scene that we bring out each year and display in the living room. The manger is always put in the very middle of this display, but we never put the baby Jesus in the manger until Christmas day. It's just a fun family tradition.

My mom started a great ritual with ornaments. Each year she buys Bethany and me a brand-new ornament that pertains to something current in our lives. For example, when I started playing golf, I got a golf ornament. When Bethany started taking ballet lessons, she received a ballerina ornament for Christmas. One year I got a baseball ornament. Another year (when I started acting), Mom got me an ornament with the two clown faces on it—you know, one is laughing and one is sad. And during our kindergarten year, we received a little desk ornament.

It's so much fun to look at all our ornaments from years past. Bethany and I really get a kick out of putting them on the tree. Mom told us that someday, when we leave home, we get to take all our ornaments with us and decorate our own family Christmas tree with them.

We also open stockings early each Christmas morning. And they're always filled with a bunch of fun little things like gum, candy, socks, or music cassettes.

Talk to your folks about making some family traditions. Try to come up with a few ideas first—then approach them. For instance, why not designate a specific night of the week as "Family Night"? You don't have to spend a lot of money or do something expensive. The goal is simply being *together*. You could eat at McDonald's, play cards, or even go to the mall together. Think about it. I promise it'll make a difference!

E: Encourage

My parents constantly encourage me to be the very best I can be. In other words, they expect the best out of me. When I know that's what they're expecting, yet also know they'll love me when I'm *not* at my best, I'm usually motivated to live up to their expectations.

But like care, encouragement is also a two-way street. Do you encourage your mom and dad? It doesn't take much. Parents love it when we do this! Why not write a short note and hide it in your dad's coat pocket or briefcase? He may find it during the most hectic part of his day. Or imagine how your mom would feel if you made her breakfast in bed one morning. And I'm not talking about something complicated. I bet she'd remember it forever if it was only a piece of toast and a glass of orange juice!

Every Mother's Day, Bethany and I get up early and do something special for Mom and Dad. Sometimes it's something as simple as what I've just described. Sometimes we've gone together and purchased a gift that we take to them.

On Mother's Day and Father's Day we both make special cards for them and try to treat them like a king and queen for the day. It's the little things, like going out of your way, that will genuinely encourage your parents.

Help! My Body's Changing

Yeah, I know. None of us likes to talk about it, but we're all having to deal with it, huh? Our changing bodies, that is. You've probably already noticed that I'm pretty short. Even though I'm almost sixteen, I could pass for a thirteen-year-old. That's discouraging. I've asked my dad how he dealt with being short. He says he just kept telling himself that someday he'd probably hit a growth spurt. And he was right! He's almost six feet tall now.

It's tough when your body is going through all kinds of puberty changes, isn't it? Sometimes it's just plain gross. But when I get down about it, I try to focus on something that really helps. Maybe it'll help you too.

I remind myself that I have to go through all these changes to get to adulthood. And since I'm looking forward to being an adult, that seems to make the awkwardness temporarily bearable. I also have to keep telling myself that I'm still in the middle of becoming. In other words, the final picture hasn't been developed yet.

Find a Few Models

I'm especially bothered when I have to stand next to a giant. It always seems to make my body seem even shorter. I find myself hoping that people really look on the inside instead of glaring at the outside package.

But you know what's made a positive difference in my perspective? Having some strong role models. Do you have any? If not, try to think of a few people you admire who can help pull you through these uncertain times.

▼ ▼ ▼ ▼ ▼

Try to keep your changing body in perspective. It may not look like it right now, but you really will turn out okay. Everyone else did!

I really admire Miami Dolphins quarterback Dan Marino. I've never met him in person, but I watch him from a distance. He seems to be down-to-earth and genuine. I want to be like that. Even when he's signing autographs, he does it with such ease.

I wonder if he struggled with all these changes during his teen years. I mean, was it hard on him? I like to think it was. Because I like to believe it's kinda tough on everyone. But I tell myself, "See—Dan turned out great. And so can you!" When I'm outside playing football, I find myself trying to mimic his throwing technique.

I also admire the assistant pastor at my church. His name is Bob Seers. He lives a consistent and genuine lifestyle. I've asked him some of my deepest questions. Things like, "What if I'm believing all the wrong stuff?" Or "How do I know the Bible is really true?"

He helped me solidify my faith and showed me how to really study the Bible. My relationship with him brought me through many uncertainties and doubts. He helped me realize that God doesn't make junk! And even though it's all kind of confusing right now (with my body and everything), God has a wonderful plan for my life. I've learned that if I keep my focus on that plan, I can make it through the uncomfortable changes.

My Advice

I realize it's easy for me to say all this stuff. It's a lot harder to accept it and actually let it help you feel better, isn't it? But I really do want to help.

I'm gonna take my last name and use it as an acrostic. (Now we'll find out who was listening in English class! Just kidding.) Maybe some of these suggestions will help.

C: Cause and Effect

Everything that's going on with your body is happening for a purpose. That's really hard to believe sometimes, huh? But it's true! Look around you. Everything in our world is based on a "cause and effect" principle. Toss something up in the air and it's going to come right back down. That's the cause and effect of gravity. Wear the same gym socks for more than five days, and the emergency team will have to surgically remove the crust from your feet. Cause and effect!

Okay, you know I'm partly kidding. But I'm partly serious too. Will it help if you'll try to accept the fact that things are just going to be really confusing for the next couple of years? I've resigned myself to it, because I realize *everything* is changing. This is a dramatic transition, isn't it? And many times it's hard to know how to deal with all the changes.

Our emotions are going outta whack. We look at the opposite sex differently now. Our hormones are waking up and trying to explode. Often it seems like there's not even an in-between; we're either super happy or super depressed. Again, cling to the fact that all the changes your body is going through are happening for a reason. Remember, cause and effect.

A: Attributes

We *all* have gifts or talents. One of mine is being pretty good at sports without having to practice at it for a long period of time. I used to love reading so much that I ignored sports altogether. My grandpa would come by and try to get me to play catch with him, but I just wasn't interested. He'd throw me the ball, and after a couple of times, I'd say, "Okay, I'm done." I wasn't even trying.

▾   ▾   ▾   ▾   ▾

I'm a sports fanatic! But I would have never known I could excel in athletics if I hadn't dared to try.

But when I was nine, I became interested in golf. My dad put a tuna can in the ground of our backyard, and I knocked golf balls into it. At that time I was using Dad's old, rusty clubs that he had sawed off for me. When my parents saw that I was interested in golf enough to work at it, they bought me an inexpensive set of clubs for my tenth birthday.

Golfing got me interested in a lot of other sports. Now, I play hockey, tennis, baseball, and football. My favorite TV station of all time is ESPN. I'm a sports fanatic! But I would have never known I could excel in athletics if I hadn't dared to try.

What are your attributes? Have you discovered them yet? If you haven't, think of these years as an exciting adventure! Dare to explore some uncharted territory. For instance, if you've never tried gymnastics, why not give it a shot? Or what about art? Ever think about offering to help make and paint the props for your school play? The possibilities are endless! And the more you find out what you can do, the better you'll feel about yourself during these weird years.

S: Special

You are unique! There is no one in the entire world just like you. So make the most of your individual personality and talents. Refuse to fall into the comparison game. When we start comparing ourselves to others, we'll always come up short! It stands to reason that there will always be someone who's better at something than we are. Why fall into that? Believe in who *you* are!

If you have to remind yourself daily that you're special, do it! Do whatever it takes to make yourself start believing it. Hang a note in your locker, memorize a favorite saying or Scripture, compliment yourself every hour under your breath, say "I am special" every night out loud before you get into bed. Be willing to invest in your self-confidence. It'll go a long way!

T: Timing

It's not much fun to develop slower or faster (physically) than those around you, is it? But we have to remember that each one of us is set on a different biological timer.

In the long run, it won't make any difference if you were smaller for a longer period of time than your friends, or if you were bigger before anyone else. I mean, ten years from now, who's going to remember besides you? Absolutely no one. So try not to let it get you down now.

That's much easier said than done when you're right in the middle of changing. I try to remember that my body is changing at the exact pace that's right for me. Yours is too. And the best part? This won't last forever! Time will soon be up, and you'll be completely developed. And chances are, you'll like what you've become!

I: Intellect

Everyone stresses how we need to develop physical co-ordination during these years, but we sometimes forget that we have a responsibility to develop our minds as well.

I have to be honest: I'd much rather be outside tossing a football around than solving geometry equations, but I realize both are important. Just as I enjoy giving sports 100 percent, I also have to strive to give my studies 100 percent.

Girls sometimes think that guys won't like them if they make good grades. Like if the guy she has a crush on notices she aces every test, he won't be attracted to her. Can I crush that myth? It's totally stupid! If there is someone who thinks less of you for using your brain, he or she isn't worth going after. A real friend encourages you to do your best.

The more we stretch our minds, the more opportunities we'll have to choose from when we graduate. So I want to encourage you to develop and use your intellect to your utmost potential. Don't sell yourself short.

L: Love

Even though it's tough during these awkward years, try to love yourself. The sooner we learn to accept ourselves (including our flaws), the stronger our self-esteem will be.

▼ ▼ ▼ ▼ ▼

**When we really start to accept
and love ourselves for who we are and
who we dream we can be, we'll begin
turning our weaknesses into strengths.**

I think of it like this: We have a choice. We can either be our own best friend and pat ourselves on the back, or we can be our own worst enemy. I used to be my biggest enemy. When I'd blow it, I tended to say negative things to myself. Stuff like, "Chris, you're so stupid! How could you have done that?" But I've slowly begun to realize that I need to be my best friend. Now when I blow it, I try to say positive things. Stuff like, "You'll do better next time. It was a tough test."

See, the more negative things we tell ourselves, the longer it takes to overcome those damaging remarks. But when we really start to accept and love ourselves for who we are and who we dream we can be, we'll begin turning our weaknesses into strengths. I'll talk more about this later in chapter 14, but start loving yourself right now. Go ahead. You're worth it!

E: Excel

Determine to be the very best you can be! You've all heard the saying, "When the going gets tough, the tough get going." I believe it's true. When hard times hit, what do you do? Giving up is easy. It's a quick cop out. Anyone can quit. It takes guts to keep going in spite of adversity. It's during these times that we grow stronger. And the stronger we become, the more we excel and rise to the top.

Don't compete with the person sitting next to you. Compete only with yourself. Strive to develop your own gifts and abilities to the very max.

Sometimes Being Recognized Means Being Unpopular

You may think that because I'm an actor, everyone loves me. *Not!* As I mentioned earlier, I went through some tough times when I was younger, and I still face some rough spots.

Because I've always had a small build, I've been pushed around a lot. And I gotta tell you, that's never been easy to handle. You know what I'm learning, though? I'm beginning to realize that if I laugh at myself, others don't have anything to laugh at. And I'm also learning that (this is a tough one) if I keep my mouth shut and don't smart off to someone who's trying to push me around, I'll more likely come out ahead than if I try to fight back.

▼　▼　▼　▼　▼

I'm beginning to realize that if I laugh at myself, others don't have anything to laugh at.

Even at Age Five

When I was in kindergarten, my doctor discovered that I had a lazy eye. He decided to cover the good eye to make the weaker eye work harder. So I had to wear a patch over my eye. You know what the kids called me? Scarecrow. I felt crushed. It confused me. I'd run home and go, "Mom, why do my friends laugh at me and tease me because of my patch? Don't they know it's from the doctor, and I have to wear it?"

I didn't make fun of anyone, therefore, it was really hard to understand why others were making fun of me. I wasn't dishing it out. I hadn't asked for it. I was friendly to my classmates.

It was then that my parents began teaching me not to get even by fighting back. They urged me to ignore the slams, and try instead to look past the words and focus on what's making them act that way. "There's a reason that they're being mean to you," Mom would say. "Maybe they don't get much love at home. So when they come to school they're angry, and they take it out on whoever's available. Right now, you're the target."

Four Eyes

When I was in the first grade, I had to get glasses. And you guessed it, kids made fun of me. After all, I was the only student in the class who had glasses. But my mom was great! She found a book that told a story of Arthur the moose who had to wear glasses. She privately asked my teacher if she would read it to the class. After that book, the kids quit making fun of my glasses. And eventually, through the months and years that followed, several of my classmates got glasses too.

Life Gets Pushy

All through elementary school, I was constantly being

pushed to the back of the line because I was so small. This was especially frustrating during lunchtime when I was hungry!

I was also one of the first kids at my school to get a retainer. It was sort of an advanced retainer. This thing was huge! Sometimes it felt like it was bigger than my whole mouth. I had to take it out just to talk or I sounded like I had a mouth full of marbles; everything was jumbled and hard to understand.

When kids started making fun of me, I decided to try to turn the tables. I took my retainer out and showed them that my name was imprinted on the inside. Instead of getting down because I was being teased, I started bragging on this retainer and acted like it was my most prized possession. You know what? That confident attitude curbed the harassment until it finally stopped altogether.

Recognize This Label?

When I was in the fourth grade, it seemed like everyone in my class had the fancy, name-brand sneakers. Mine were usually from Target or something like that. My mom felt that since my feet were growing so fast, it would be a waste of money to buy expensive shoes that I could only wear for a couple of months. She knew I'd never wear them out. We had to buy a new pair every few months because of the rate at which I was growing.

But again, kids always made fun of what I was wearing. My tennis shoes had Velcro straps on them instead of laces. I liked that because I could put them on and be ready to go faster than those with shoes that tied. And at that time I was into a "the faster the better" philosophy because it meant I could get outside and start playing sooner.

We had a school dance, and I wore my Velcro tennis shoes. Everyone at the dance laughed and made fun of me. To this day, I still remember the bad feelings I had. It really hurt!

I ran home and cried. Mom hugged me and said,

"Chris, it's really hard for me to see you get hurt like this, but the reality of life is that kids are cruel." Then she wiped my eyes and hugged me again while continuing to talk. "It's a fact of life that you'll be hurt again. And again. And again. But Chris, it's not your problem, it's theirs. Anyone who makes fun of someone else has something very sad going on inside of him."

That was an important lesson. A hard lesson, but an important one. Today when someone makes fun of me, I remember Mom's words: "Something very sad is going on inside of him." That helps me look beyond the cruel remarks and see him in a different light.

Being Recognized

As mentioned earlier, when I'm on hiatus from *Step by Step*, I go to regular school. You might think because I'm on a TV show that everyone wants to be my friend, but that's just not true. Some people are jealous. Occasionally, a few of the students act rude or sarcastic to me when I say something. Others make fun of me or think I'm stuck-up.

I think sometimes actors are treated more cruelly than the average kid. It's like people have this preconceived idea of who I'm supposed to be, or who I think I am. Since I'm an actor, many automatically assume I'm a brat. They treat me like, "Who do you think you are?" And I think to myself, *Nobody. Just Chris going to class.* These are the kids who have an attitude about me even before they've actually met me!

It's hard. Sometimes when kids *do* want to become my friend, they only like me because they think I make a lot of money or they try to talk me into somehow getting them on the show. (Yeah, right. Like I could do that!) And some want to know if I can get them an autograph from one of my fellow actors.

▼ ▼ ▼ ▼ ▼

I'm really thankful for my good friends. They like me just because I'm me. Nothing more. Nothing less. That's real friendship.

There are a few, though, who are genuine. And I'm really thankful for my good friends. They're the ones who don't care if I'm ever on TV or in another movie the rest of my life. They like me just because I'm me. Nothing more. Nothing less. *That's* real friendship.

Hey, I'm Not Perfect!

Being from California, I'm used to warm weather all year. One particular weekend, my mom and I were in Montana while filming *Beethoven's 2nd*. It was a lot colder there, and we went to the mall so I could get some warm clothes.

I was in this clothing store trying on stuff and these guys recognized me from *Step by Step*. They started making fun of me and calling me a nerd. I wanted to scream, "Hey, gimme a break! I'm just trying on some clothes. Leave me alone." But I didn't.

I do play sort of a nerd on *Step*. Unfortunately, many people assume I'm like that in real life. Actually, Mark Foster and I are total opposites. I enjoy playing that character, but I'm really not like him at all. I do well in school, but I have to work at it a little harder than Mark does.

Another time, we celebrated my sister's birthday by giving her an ice-skating party. It was a huge rink, and I'd only ice-skated a few times in my life. But I was out there in the middle of all the action, giving it all I had. A group of kids recognized me and started following me while making rude comments about the way I skated. Again, it hurt. I felt like shouting, "Hey, just let me skate like anyone else!" Instead, I didn't say anything.

Strangers usually don't have an opportunity to see me

perform well in a sport because I'm not currently playing a role that requires athletic ability. The truth is, though, I'm crazy about sports. I'm currently taking karate lessons. I love to snow ski, snorkel, ride bikes, swim, and go horse-back riding. I love just about anything you can do out-doors.

My Family, My Friends

Actors don't always get to show their true colors. Think about it. If we're having a bad day and we show it, we run the risk of others automatically assuming we're always that way. Or we run the risk of the tabloids picking up on something we might have said or done. No actor wants that! So when I'm having a hard day, I try to keep it inside . . . at least until I get home.

Once I'm with my family, I can really relax and be myself. That's one reason my family is so important to me. They understand, when I'm going through a tough time, that it'll pass. They give me slack. They have created a safe atmosphere in which I feel free to express myself. And really, isn't that what every home should be like, whether you're an actor or not?

Turning Weaknesses into Strengths

I know I've mentioned this already, but for me it's a major issue: my height. I'm probably a little too self-conscious about it. I guess it's because I've been pushed around a lot. Everyone has something he wishes he could change about himself. For you, it might be your nose, your weight, your teeth, or your complexion.

You know what I'm beginning to realize, though? We can take the things we don't like about ourselves and use them to work for us!

Here's What I Did

I decided to use my height—or lack of it—to my advantage. Obviously I can't dunk a basketball, so I took up golf. Since I'm short, I'm a lot closer to the ball, and I can swing hard.

In baseball, the advantage of my height comes in handy when I'm going for a ground ball. Again, because I'm short I'm that much closer to the ground!

We play a lot of street football in my neighborhood. There are some pretty good-sized kids who like to play, and usually the linemen are huge. But because I'm so short, most of the time the defensive linemen don't even know where I am. It's hilarious!

And on the Screen

In the entertainment business, a short stature can really benefit an actor. My lack of height works to my advantage because I can play younger roles and stay in them for a greater period of time. For instance, if a show has the choice of casting two equally talented sixteen-year-old guys for a show that they want to run for at least three years, many times they'll select the sixteen-year-old actor who could pass for a thirteen-year-old. This ensures the producers that when the sixteen-year-old is actually twenty, he could still pass for sixteen or seventeen. This is how they "grow up" kids on a show.

▼ ▼ ▼ ▼ ▼

When people make fun of me because of my height, my response is, "Fine—I get paid to be short."

I've often played characters who are younger than my actual age. The youngest I've played is three years younger than my real age. So when people make fun of me because of my height, my response is, "Fine—I get paid to be short."

What about You?

Again, everyone has something he wishes were different about his physique or facial features. The trick is learning to accept those things about yourself then working them to your advantage.

Sly Stallone, Michael J. Fox, and Dustin Hoffman are all fairly short. But they've overcome. Instead of wishing they could be something they're not, they've used their lack of height to their advantage.

What if Barbra Streisand had said, "I might as well forget a singing career. My nose is too big. No one would want to see *me* sing!"

Or what if Cindy Crawford had said, "I'll only model in my dreams. I've got this mole by my lip that's just wrecking everything."

We would have been denied some beautiful music and some great modeling if they had taken that attitude, wouldn't we? Talk-show hostess Oprah Winfrey has been open about her struggle with weight. The issue really isn't how much she weighs, or how she took it off, or the marathon she ran. The real issue is that she became successful in spite of what she didn't like about herself. I don't know what it is about *you* that you're struggling with right now, but will you accept my challenge to simply accept yourself? Seek different ways of using what you don't like to benefit instead of limit yourself.

It's an Expensive Lesson

Many people *never* learn to accept their weaknesses or flaws. And because they're unhappy, they tend to make everyone around them miserable as well. And others go through life spending a fortune trying to create the perfect body, as if chasing a dream.

Talk-show hostess Jenny Jones once hosted a panel of guests who had gone through extensive surgeries to change the parts of their bodies they weren't satisfied with. One guest was nicknamed Barbie, because she had spent over $50,000 trying to look just like a Barbie doll!

It was incredible! The camera focused on a Barbie doll, then threw a freeze-frame of the Barbie look-alike right next to it. They sported the same clothes, same hair color, and same body shape. The woman really did look just like the doll!

But when Jenny began taking questions from the studio audience, one lady stood and addressed Barbie. She said, "Haven't you stopped to think about what you'll look like in ten years? I mean, you're a duplicate right now, but your body, like every body, will eventually start to sag and wear. What will you do then? Spend even more money trying to stay caught up with the perfect look?"

The guest hadn't thought that far in advance. All she could think of was the immediate present. It was sad that an entire panel of people were willing to go on national television and share what they didn't like about themselves and talk freely about the huge sum of money they had willingly shelled out to become "perfect."

It's Only a Dream

No matter how much money we can offer, we'll never have the perfect body. Face it, for 99 percent of the human population, that's just a dream. Still, people line up by the hundreds for having bags removed from underneath their eyes, liposuction, putting dimples in or taking dimples out, tummy tucks . . . You name it, and you can get it done with the right amount of money. But as soon as you do, you'll probably notice something else you'd like to have changed. When does it end?

The answer, again, is learning to accept ourselves *just as we are,* and striving to turn what we don't like about ourselves into our assets. Did you know that years ago when Arnold Schwarzenegger was only a bodybuilder trying to break into acting, he was turned down for three reasons?

▼ ▼ ▼ ▼ ▼

The answer is learning to accept ourselves just as we are, and striving to turn what we don't like about ourselves into our assets.

He was first told that his body was too muscular and

big, almost awkward, to be a successful actor. (What were they thinking, right?) Next, he was told that it was too hard to understand him when he spoke. His foreign accent was too thick. It was then suggested that he change his name. Arnold—sounds like a nerd. And Schwarzenegger? Not something that flows easily.

But you know what happened, don't you? He didn't give up. He could have. It probably would have been easier to simply quit and conclude, *I guess they're right.*

But he began working to trim down his muscular body. He was still muscular, but a lot lighter. He also began working to improve his speech and enunciation. He took time to study the English language. He *didn't,* however, change his name. And I'm glad he didn't. It serves to remind us that if we work hard enough we *can* turn our "flaws" (or the things we don't like about ourselves) into our assets.

The Bottom Line

So what it all comes down to is your attitude. You can become bitter about those who make fun of whatever it is you don't like about yourself, or you can accept yourself and determine to become the best you can be. Now, we're not talking about shelling out big bucks to chase a flimsy dream, are we? No way! We're talking about liking ourselves and allowing that confidence to show up in our lifestyle. And that is mighty hard to beat!

The Opposite Sex

In my short history (whoops—no pun intended!) with girls, I've come to a few conclusions.

What I've Learned

Many times girls like older guys. This can be pretty frustrating for us guys who are simply trying to get the attention of the girls in our class.

I think I understand the reason, but it's still frustrating. I guess the reason so many girls are attracted to older guys is because they tend to mature about two years earlier than guys do. This means that girls are about two years beyond most guys their age.

So, naturally, a guy who's a couple of years older will have better-developed listening skills, be a better conversationalist, and generally be more comfortable around the opposite sex.

What I Don't Understand

I guess there are some things guys will never figure out

about girls. For instance, they're always saying how they just want to be really good friends with guys. But many times when we *do* reach out and try to start a friendship, they go bonkers. All of a sudden they panic and think we're "after" them.

What I Think

We're flooded with pressure today to act older than we really are, and most of this pressure comes from the media. When viewing any kind of love story that involves teens on the big screen, it's the norm to see them engaged in a physically close relationship with the opposite sex.

This gives us a false message! First of all, there's the pressure to live up to what we see, and second, there's a *big* difference between being *physically* ready and *emotionally* ready. It doesn't take a man to give in to the pressure of his hormones. It does, however, take a man to put his own desires on hold and wait for a lifetime commitment in marriage.

What I Want

The kind of girl I enjoy spending time with is one who has strong morals. I admire young ladies who care enough about themselves to set guidelines and live out their values.

▼ ▼ ▼ ▼ ▼

I plan to abstain from sex until I'm married; therefore, I'm attracted to someone who shares that same determination.

I plan to abstain from sex until I'm married; therefore I'm attracted to someone who shares that same determination. I also enjoy girls who share my love of sports. None of us enjoys being around someone who's just like us, but when establishing a relationship, it is nice to spend time with someone who shares some of your same interests.

Dating Guidelines

Can you imagine being on a football team and not having a game plan? Picture it: You're running out to join your other teammates on the field; the whistle is blown, and you have no strategy. Chances are good your team won't win.

I think it works the same way in relationships. To have quality relationships with the opposite sex, we need a game plan. Too many times we jump into dating without even thinking it through first. And really, the whole dating game can be kind of complex.

My parents are helping me create a solid game plan, one that will help me succeed instead of fail. For instance, they want to help me with the decision I've made to remain sexually pure until marriage. So the first date I ever went on was with my parents.

Now, hold on! Before you turn the page and start thinking, *Your parents? This is too weird!* give me a chance, okay?

A Lifetime Memory

Before I started dating, Mom and Dad gave me one of the most meaningful nights of my entire life. On my fifteenth birthday, we all got dressed up and they treated me to an incredible dinner at a special restaurant. My sister, Bethany, wasn't allowed to come. She'll get her first date with Mom and Dad when she turns fifteen. Anyway, it was just the three of us. I felt pretty special. They had gone to a lot of trouble to plan this evening just for me.

The waiter brought out a juicy steak cooked just the way I like it. Throughout the dinner, Mom and Dad talked about their dating life. I already knew how and where they met and all that stuff. But it was kind of neat to hear the highlights all over again—with just the three of us. It was like they were giving me an extremely personal peek into their private lives.

Both of my parents have expressed their desire for me to remain sexually pure until marriage. We talked about the pressure I would encounter when I started dating, and how I'd hear friends laughing or bragging about how far they'd gone with a girl. They told me it would be tough, but because the Bible is clear on sexual involvement outside of marriage, they expected me to live by its truth.

▼ ▼ ▼ ▼ ▼

Because the Bible is clear on sexual involvement outside of marriage, they expected me to live by its truth.

We also talked about all the other reasons it just makes sense to wait. The fact that there are now over fifty sexually transmitted diseases (STDs) and that the spreading of AIDS has reached epidemic proportions makes it seem stupid to be involved sexually outside of a lifetime commitment.

What They Say

Yeah, I know all the talk about safe sex and how wearing a condom will supposedly guarantee you and your partner's safety. But I'm not falling for that. The AIDS virus is actually 450 times smaller than a sperm! Safe sex? Even the experts say it's like water going through a net.

And in movies and TV, sex is often seen as what's simply expected in any dating relationship. It's very rare that the media is really honest with its viewers. The media won't show us a girl who's crying after her first sexual experience because she no longer has her virginity. And we're not going to see what a guy has to go through after he's contracted an STD. We don't see the emptiness, the aloneness, and the lousy self-esteem. What we do see are professional actors making out in smooth, sensual scenes. They look comfortable with each other, and they move with grace.

You know why? *They're acting!* See, that's the lie. In real life it's just not like that. And this is what Mom and Dad were trying to explain to me on my fifteenth birthday. Anyone can make sex look smooth and great on the screen. But that's not real. Real is waking up next to someone with bad breath and loving them in spite of it. Real is being awkward and learning together how to be smooth. And real is loving each other more and more in spite of the first few embarrassing stages of unfamiliarity.

Great sex takes time, I was told. And commitment. And an awful lot of security between you and your partner that says, "We're going to love each other the rest of our lives." See, in that kind of security, a couple has the exciting opportunity of learning *together* what makes great sex.

Here's the bottom line for me: I don't want my honeymoon to seem like two pros who have had an incredible amount of practice. I want *my* honeymoon to consist of two amateurs who are learning together for the first time how to really please one another—two amateurs who are committed to spending the rest of their lives in a marriage relationship that revolves around the other person's needs.

My Commitment

Too idealistic, you think? Well, I admit, I'm aiming high. But see, that's what I want for my life. And I have a right to cling to those decisions and values, don't I? Just as you have a right to cling to what you want.

I'm the first to admit that it's not smooth sailing. As stated earlier in the chapter, there's an incredible amount of pressure today to "put out." If I were unsupported in this decision, it might be close to impossible, but that's where Mom and Dad come in. Back to my fifteenth birthday, okay? We're talking about all this stuff while I'm chowing down on that juicy steak. And Mom and Dad have expressed their expectations for me to live an abstinent lifestyle until marriage.

(Hey, before you start thinking it's unfair of them to put that kind of guideline on me, I probably need to tell you that I *like* it that my parents expect the best of me. It gives me confidence to realize they dream big for me. It makes me want to expect the best of myself!)

▼ ▼ ▼ ▼ ▼

I like it that my parents expect the best of me. It gives me confidence to realize they dream big for me. It makes me want to expect the best of myself!

So, we've just finished those juicy steaks, I've had about four refills on my Sprite, and Mom pulls out this really cool package. It's wrapped really special, know what I mean? Not just the birthday paper you can buy at the store and do yourself, but the *professional* kind. I can tell this one's been store-wrapped.

Mom hands it to me, and Dad says, "Chris, not only do we expect you to live by God's plan regarding sex, but that's also *our* plan too."

Then Mom says, "Even though you haven't started to date yet, you will soon. And you'll probably date several girls before you fall in love with the one you want to marry. This commitment to stay sexually pure won't always be easy."

"But remember, Chris," my dad said, "we expect the

best of you. We expect you to be a man and say no to the desires within you until you're married. And son, you're not in this alone. You have our support."

"And to remind you of our support," Mom said, "we're giving you this special gift, tonight, on your very first date, to be a consistent reminder of how much we believe in you."

I unwrapped the gift. You know what it was? It was a simple, yet classy, signature ring. "Chris," Dad said, "we want this ring to be a reminder for you."

"Let it help you remember your decision to remain sexually pure until marriage," Mom said. "When you're out with a girl and you're holding hands, you're going to feel this ring against your skin. And it's going to remind you to set limits."

"And when you're kissing a girl good night," Dad said, "this ring will serve as a reminder that you're building physical boundaries."

Wow! I can't even express to you—because I don't really have the words—how incredibly important that ring is to me. But even more important is what Mom said next.

"Chris, on your wedding night, take this ring and give it to your wife. Explain that you have kept yourself sexually pure for her and her alone. Place it in her hands," she said. "And as you wrap her fingers around it, tell her that it's hers to keep . . . until your own son or daughter's fifteenth birthday. Explain that you want her to present this very special gift to your own child some-day."

So, Here's What I'm Thinking

You know what that tells me? It makes me think that the most important gift I can ever give my wife is my virginity. It's priceless. Once it's gone, it's gone forever. Even though I don't have a clue who I'll marry someday, I do know this: I respect myself enough to know that I want to look at her with integrity and be able to give to her and her alone the best gift I can give—my virginity.

Someday when I'm on my honeymoon, I don't want to be comparing my wife with everyone else I've been with. That'd be a killer! And I don't want her comparing me with anyone else. So, it just makes sense to wait.

Back to the Game Plan

Remember that analogy we talked about? You know, the football team who would lose the game because they didn't have a plan? Well, let's get back to our dating strategy. Since I've made such a big commitment, it's obvious I have to have a well thought-out plan ahead of time to help me maintain my decision.

▼ ▼ ▼ ▼ ▼

I can't bring a girl into our house if Mom and Dad are gone.

Again, Mom and Dad are helping me with this. They've given me some guidelines, and I'm adding some of my own. Here's a quick taste of what I'm talking about:

First, I can't bring a girl into our house if Mom and Dad are gone. At least one parent has to be there, or our home is off-limits to my date. The reason? When no adults are around, there's a much greater chance I may want to see what I can get away with. Why set myself up? If I'm serious about sticking to the decision I've made, I have to be realistic. And reality tells me that if I'm alone with a girl in an empty house, I'll feel the temptation much more than I would if we weren't alone.

Second, I should look for someone with similar beliefs. I've talked about this a little already. But again, if I'm determined to keep the commitment I've made regarding sexual purity, why would I choose to date someone who simply wants me to "put out"? That kind of girl is usually looking for something that's missing in her own life, like love from her father.

Dad told me once that girls who are really "easy" *usually* (I'm emphasizing *usually,* okay?) don't have a healthy relationship with their dad. He says that girls receive a healthy concept about their womanhood from their father. And if a girl doesn't have a dad, or if her dad doesn't affirm her in the right way and help her feel good about becoming a lady, she'll often keep trying to find that love in relationships. The sad thing is, she'll usually mistake sex for love.

Because she was never close to her father, she'll try to get physically close to as many men as possible . . . trying to fill that void in her life. And most of the time, she won't even realize that's what she's trying to do.

Again, I'm saying *usually* here because I know that's not always true. And I'm certainly *not* saying that every girl who doesn't have a dad is easy. (If you're a girl and you're reading this and feeling pretty ticked right now, please go back and reread what I've said. Okay?)

If I choose to date girls who respect my decision for sexual purity, and girls who have made that decision themselves, our chances of becoming sexually involved with each other will be less.

Third, I should look for someone with similar beliefs. Because I believe in a healthy lifestyle, I want to date a girl who also believes in taking care of her body. I don't smoke, and I don't drink. Not just because I'm underage or some goody-two-shoes—I make plenty of mistakes. But I do care about keeping my body healthy. Therefore, I want to date girls who believe their bodies are valuable enough to stay away from destructive things.

Finally, I should plan out my dates ahead of time. Too often people let down their guard because they didn't have a strategy. Part of my game plan is simply to *have* a plan. I want us to plan the evening *before* we go out. I'm not talking about a minute-by-minute time schedule. I'm talking about knowing where we're going and what we're going to do.

▼　▼　▼　▼　▼

It only makes sense that we plan ahead of time what we'll be doing so we won't end up with a couple of hours of temptation on our hands.

For instance, if she doesn't have to be home until 1:00 A.M., and the movie's over at 10:30, and we've already had dinner . . . we've got two and a half hours on our hands. And, like the football team who lost the game because they had no direction, I want to do everything I can to ensure I keep my commitment.

It only makes sense, then, that we plan ahead of time what we'll be doing so we won't end up with a couple of hours of temptation on our hands.

This Isn't the Final Word

I'm only fifteen, so it's obvious I don't have all the answers about dating. I won't even start to date until I'm sixteen. Oh, I've done a few group things like head over to Taco Bell after school for a while, but I don't consider that real dating.

I know I'll probably start with a lot of group dating. First of all, being in a *group* with the opposite sex is a lot more comfortable than being *alone* with the opposite sex. I need to learn a few things first, like basically getting comfortable, and not worrying about what I'm going to say. You know, stuff like that.

Second, being in a group guarantees a lot less opportunity to let down my guard. I'm determined to keep that commitment, remember? So, I'm going to do everything I can to be in situations that will help strengthen my decision rather than weaken it.

That's my game plan. What's your strategy? If you don't have one yet, I encourage you to develop one. If your parents can't or won't help you, borrow some of these ideas. Seriously—I'd love to share them with you!

What's Really Important

I get some pretty cool perks every now and then because I'm an actor, and even though I enjoy all that stuff, the bottom line is that *things* can all be taken away in a flash. What's ultimately important to me are the things that can never be taken away from me.

I Believe . . .

As mentioned in chapter 10, my parents have taught me that my security must be settled in something that's not fleeting—something that won't change with the ratings. That something is my personal faith in God.

I'm accepted for who I am, instead of what others want me to be. My own dad forgives me when I blow it—just like God does. My parents don't always like what I do, but they'll never stop loving me.

It blows my mind to think that the Creator of the universe—the one who created *me*—knows me better than anyone (including my family) and yet still loves me more than anyone else in the world! That gives me a ton of security.

▼　▼　▼　▼　▼

**It blows my mind to think that the Creator of
the universe—the one who created me—
knows me better than anyone and yet still
loves me more than anyone else in the world!**

See, it doesn't matter if our ratings go down or if our show is canceled or if I lose a part I really want. Though those things would hurt, they won't destroy me . . . because my self-esteem comes from God. My faith in God is what makes me want to do my best each day. He's made such a positive difference in my life that I want to turn around and make an impact on the lives of *others*.

I'm Not Alone

From time to time a professional athlete, actor, or musician will speak out concerning his or her faith. Thousands of celebrities have voiced their religious convictions, and you're probably aware of many. Though my purpose is not to mention everyone I can think of who falls into that category, I do want to focus on something I read recently.

There was an article in a recent issue of *TV Guide* on Kirk Cameron, who played the role of Mike Seaver in ABC's *Growing Pains* for several years. I thought it was interesting that his costar Joanna Kerns, who played his mom on *Growing Pains,* noticed his religious faith. She said, "Kirk is a very unusual person with a commitment to living on what he interprets to be a higher plane. He had opinions that were far more conservative than the rest of the cast's, and sometimes that rubbed the wrong way. But his intention," she said, "has always been to attain that higher self. It was an odd thing to see in a child" (*TV Guide,* 18 February 1995).

Gimme a Break!

I can't help but wonder how she would have commented if he'd been on drugs or sleeping around. It seems that has almost become commonplace among teens, and when any of us strives to live above that and place our trust in a higher power than ourselves, it makes people nervous.

Joanna didn't stop there. She went on to say, "He found a set of values that he will not deviate from. It cuts out a lot of opportunities for him because he won't do certain types of movies."

Kirk wants to be involved in positive projects. What's wrong with that? "There's a lot to do," he says, "but not a lot of what *I* want to do."

I think it's easy to accept the compromising roles. Scripts are full of them, and actors are bombarded with them. It takes a lot more strength to be selective. I feel the same way Kirk does. I want to make a positive difference in people's lives. Part of that is related to my faith, and part of it is simply because I have higher goals for my life than doing work for work's sake.

At the end of the article, Kirk said, "People can write me off and figure, 'Oh, he's hiding something.' But Chelsea [Kirk's wife] and I have a million choices to make every day, and we don't want to overlook things because they seem too idealistic."

People often think I'm too idealistic or conservative simply because I'm trying not to compromise my faith and my values. We've become accustomed to hearing bad press on the wrong choices teen actors have made—a sexually promiscuous lifestyle, a mismanagement of finances, a rebellious attitude, or substance abuse. But when teen actors receive bad press because of *good* choices they're making, I want to scream, "Give me a break!"

So What's It All Mean?

See, I don't want to be someone who just sort of flits through the world. I want my life to matter! I want the choices I make to benefit others in a positive way. I'm aggressive—in a good way. I'm determined to be the very best that I can possibly be.

▼ ▼ ▼ ▼ ▼

A personal mission takes thought, planning, and careful strategy. It's different from goal setting.

The only way I can achieve that is by thinking really hard about my direction. I'm in the process of developing a "personal mission" for my life. Yeah, I know, it sounds kind of "old" and "adultish," but I only have one life, and I'm serious about how I want it to turn out. A personal mission takes thought, planning, and careful strategy. It's different from goal setting. Some of my goals are to be a terrific actor, improve my golf game, and get a solid education. But my mission reveals what my life revolves around. Every decision I make and action I take should reflect it.

So what *is* my personal mission? Well, I'm still working on it, but part of it is to make a positive difference in the lives of those around me. Everything I do, therefore, should help accomplish that.

The roles I accept, how I treat others, and the way I live my life should all point to making a positive difference in others. That's one reason I'm writing this book—it helps me *live* my personal mission. If the words on these pages cause even a few kids to make some good changes in their lives, I'm contributing to making a positive difference.

What about You?

Have you ever established goals for your life? What's *your* purpose? Do you want to matter to those around you? A great place to start is by simply setting some goals for yourself.

What do you want out of life? What are your strengths? What are your weaknesses? (Answering these questions helps you establish goals.) Are you willing to work on turning your liabilities into assets? How do you plan to do this? (Now you're developing a strategy.)

Once you've established some goals, take some time to think about what's ultimately important to you. Beyond achievement, recognition, or feel-good stuff . . . what *really* matters? Be willing to talk to some trusted adults (your parents, your pastor or priest, a school counselor or teacher, your coach), and get their input. Discuss with them what you want your life's personal statement to be. Tell them about your goals. They may have some valuable insight that will help you clarify your thoughts.

The Final Results

I guess the bottom line for all of us is that we want to get the very most out of life that we can. For me, that means putting a lot *into* life. The more I contribute, the better I'll feel about myself. But the things I want to contribute are those things that can't be taken away from a person: hope, faith, affirmation. Where do I get those things to give? It all comes back to my faith in God, because that can never be taken from me. It gives me the strength and security to tell others about what I've found.

Stuff No One Knows (Till Now)

You probably know by now (because you're getting close to the end of the book) that I can't do everything I want to. I have rules I'm required to live by—guidelines I choose to live by. The following stuff isn't something I talk about all the time . . . in fact, I don't think I've ever really shared this with *anyone* until now. But stick with me, and I'll clue you in on some things that may surprise you.

What I ~~Watch~~ Don't Watch

I mentioned earlier that I'm not allowed to watch R-rated movies. My parents are also pretty selective about what I can see on TV too. I never watch *Melrose Place,* and I've only seen *Beverly Hills 90210* twice. I got to watch it those times because a fellow actress was on it.

I know you probably think all this is pretty strict, and a few years ago I didn't understand it either. But the older I get, the more I'm learning that there really are reasons behind most rules.

See, I'm learning that whatever goes into my head will eventually come out. It's the ol' "garbage in/garbage out" equation. It only makes sense to assume that if I fill my mind with trash, it'll eventually begin to affect my lifestyle.

▼ ▼ ▼ ▼ ▼

I'm learning that whatever goes into my head will eventually come out. It's the ol' "garbage in/garbage out" equation.

If I sit around watching a bunch of sex-filled shows, it stands to reason I'm going to be thinking about everything I saw for the next few weeks. I'm working real hard to keep my mind clean. But it takes a lot of work and discipline.

My family doesn't even get cable TV, because if we had it, we'd watch it. We want to interact with each other more or be active outside doing something fun and physical. We don't want to be huddled around a television set.

It's Like This

My parents never wanted "show biz" to change who I am and who they're striving to help me become. They keep me humble. They make sure I know that I still have to love others. I still have to be polite. I can't make demands.

They've helped me realize that I really don't deserve *any* of this. I'm on the same level as everyone else. The recognition, the perks, and the money are all gifts that can be removed at any moment.

My family doesn't want to live with a brat, so they take great precautions to remind me of where I came from. That's easy to remember because we're all still in the same place! And if I don't follow their rules, I'm disciplined like any other kid.

Sometimes I'm grounded from my computer for a week; other times it's the Game Boy or the television. The main thing I get in trouble for is talking disrespectfully.

Just the other day I was grounded to my room. I couldn't use anything electronic. I was allowed to come out for dinner, then had to go right back to my bedroom. I deserved it; I'd had a rotten attitude toward my mom and had treated her badly.

My Possessions

I've already talked about the fact that I don't know how much money I have. But many times people assume that since I have some money (probably more than most teens my age), I also have a lot of possessions.

Well, let me fill you in. I do have a View Cam, but it was a gift from someone on *Step*. Another year, someone on the show gave me a really cool telephone. Even though lots of kids my age have their own private lines, I don't. In fact, I don't really even have the phone. Well, I *have* it . . . but I'm not using it. Mom and Dad don't want me spending all my time gabbing, so it's up in the closet until I'm a little older.

I enjoy a few extra benefits now and then, but I'm not saturated with free stuff. Occasionally I'll get some warm-up clothes or shoes from an athletic distributor, because they realize if I wear those to a charity event it's free publicity for them. And once in a while, I might get into an amusement park for free because of a special event, but it doesn't really happen that often.

Other Misconceptions

People assume I always receive the best treatment and fly first class whenever I travel anywhere. The truth is, I'm in the coach section more than anywhere else. Once in a while, a sponsoring organization will send me a first-class ticket, but it's not that often.

Many actors live in huge, fancy mansions, and you might think I'm no exception—but actually, I am. I said earlier that we've lived in the same house for years. It's comfortable, but it's nothing to get excited about. It's 1,500 square feet with three bedrooms. And no, we don't have a pool or a hot tub in the backyard.

People sometimes assume I sign autographs all the time. I *do* sign quite a few, but I don't sign as many as Sasha Mitchell, Patrick Duffy, or Suzanne Somers. I don't mind signing them at all, but after the first few hundred, my hand cramps up.

▼   ▼   ▼   ▼   ▼

Being on a sitcom is like working a full-time job while juggling homework and the rest of my life.

Another misconception people often have is that my life is easy. I think I've already alluded to the fact that I really enjoy what I do. So, yeah, I'm having a lot of fun, but I'm also working hard at it. I usually put in a nine and one-half hour day. Being on a sitcom is like working a full-time job while juggling homework and the rest of my life.

I guess people tend to assume a lot of these things because of what's printed in the tabloids. Also, when some actors brag about what they have, people assume that all actors experience the same benefits. But the truth is, we actually have a lot more in common with people who don't act than you realize. We're just like you. We have chores, bills, responsibilities, and bad days filled with rotten attitudes. But hopefully like you, we try to rise above the pressure. Sound familiar? Welcome to the club of everyday life!

Most Frequently Asked Questions

I'm asked a lot of the same questions over and over, so I thought I'd go ahead and answer them in case you're wondering some of the same things.

Do you record each one of your shows?

I don't, but my dad does. He and Mom are keeping a "library" of the work I've done. I'll probably get a good laugh out of it someday when I want to dig through the trunk and give my own kids something to do on a rainy day.

What's it like to work with . . . Sasha Mitchell . . . Suzanne Somers . . . Patrick Duffy?

Sasha's always telling me to listen to my mom. Like if she says I can't have a donut, and I try to sneak one, he's right there smiling and saying, "Chris, listen to your mom." And he's always been very respectful to her. He used to call her Mrs. Castile all the time until she finally said, "Sasha, you don't have to do this! Please, call me Donna."

All three are not only terrific actors but wonderful people as well. I'm privileged to get to work with them. (For more information, flip ahead to chapter 19.)

How much money do you make?

As I said earlier, my parents have chosen not to reveal that figure to me. Most of it goes into a trust fund that I can't get until I'm twenty-one years old anyway. I'm glad they decided a long time ago not to tell me what kind of numbers I deal with. This way I can honestly say, "I don't know" to the people who ask me this question.

Not knowing also keeps me normal . . . you know, it makes it harder for me to get a big head. Mom has always said that I'm no better or more special than anyone else simply because I'm acting. Everyone has different gifts. Just because I make money exercising my gift doesn't put me on a higher plane than other teens my age.

When you think about it, it's kind of a nervy question. I mean, how many people do you approach with that question? Would you ask your doctor, teacher, or dentist that?

Can you get me on the show?

No, I can't. I'm merely one actor among several. Can you imagine the confusion that would break out if every actor on the show brought a friend to work and said, "Can't he just have a few lines? He's my best friend"?

Roles have to be earned. And that usually involves an agent and a few auditions.

Do you like signing autographs?

I really don't mind it. It's an honor to realize that others think enough of you to actually want your signature. If I can, I try to make time to stop and sign things when I'm asked. I know how much it means to me when *I* get someone's autograph I've been wanting.

Are you really like your *Step by Step* character, Mark Foster?

No, I'm not. Mark is totally inept at sports. By this point in the book, you know I'm a sports nut! We did one episode a few years ago where Mark wanted to be on the Little League baseball team that Frank coaches. I had to act like I couldn't even throw the ball. And I had to swing the bat real crazy too. It was fun playing the part, but I hope people don't think I'm like that in real life.

I've also been told that I have a great sense of humor. People often comment on my ability to make others laugh. Mark Foster isn't like that at all!

Do all the kids on *Step by Step* get along?

Yes, we do. We kid each other a lot and actually enjoy each other's company. We don't always do things together outside of work, and because I live the farthest away, it's difficult for me to get together. But because of our tight schedule, we're together four or five days each week for several hours during our filming season.

It's fun to see the little changes each one goes through. I mean, think about it—when you're on a show for four or five years, you really grow up together.

Does Sasha Mitchell (Cody Lambert) really talk like that?

Yes, he does. He's a total blast to be around. That's his real laugh too. Unlike his character, though, he's very intellectual, whereas on the show he's sometimes portrayed as not so bright.

Where are your glasses?

I have glasses, but I don't have to wear them all the time. When I'm not wearing my glasses, it's amazing how many people still recognize me. It does take them a little longer to realize I'm the kid from the *Beethoven* movies and *Step by Step,* but they do recognize me.

Is Steve Urkel really a nerd?

No, he's not. If you've been a fan of *Family Matters,* you've probably seen a few episodes where he's played himself at the end of the show. For instance, they did one episode on violence. Laura Winslow was attacked by a gang member on the school grounds. After the show, Jaleel White (Steve Urkel) spoke into the camera as himself and offered advice on avoiding violence.

They did another episode in which a student at their high school had to have a bone marrow transplant. Again, at the end of the program, Jaleel White himself gave information on being a donor.

You may have also caught him on a few specials during the past couple of years. The voice he uses as Steve Urkel isn't his real voice. He sort of throws it up an octave to achieve the nerdy effect.

How can I get into acting?

This is probably the question I'm asked most. Here are my suggestions:

First, be as active as you can right now! Don't wait to be discovered—that idea is sort of a myth. Start getting all the acting experience you can right where you are. Does your school have speech and drama? Sign up! Audition for your school play.

What about your city? Do you have community theater? If so, call and get information on the plays they plan to produce for the next year. Ask about auditions and find out exactly what's involved. For instance, will you be expected to do a cold reading, or do they want you to come with something already prepared? Will you have to sing too?

If you need to have something prepared ahead of time, go to the library and check out some well-known plays. Find a scene, memorize it, and block it. Learn how to put yourself into the role and make the character come to life!

Do you live close to the local television stations in your area? Call and ask about locally filmed commercials. Do they accept open auditions? If so, can you put your name on the waiting list? Or could you attend a filming to see how it's done?

Second, take acting lessons. Instead of waiting around for something to happen, check the Yellow Pages for information on acting lessons. Learn all you can. This will help you become comfortable in doing several different things in front of a crowd. Develop skills in improvisation and ad-libbing (making it up as you go).

Third, find an agent. Professional actors need an agent, but how do you get one? Many people contact the Screen Actors Guild in Southern California for a listing of agents. But *never* pay money up front for an agent. A reputable agent doesn't take a fee until he or she has actually helped you land an acting role.

I'll be honest with you. If you don't live in or near L.A., Chicago, New York, or Washington, D.C., your chances are pretty slim of getting an L.A. agent. That's simply because auditions are frequently held in these major cities. So if you're living in Cheyenne, Wyoming, you probably won't be able to get an L.A. agent. What good would it do him or her? If an audition comes up in Hollywood tomorrow morning, who's he going to call . . . someone in Wyoming or someone in Pasadena? Obviously, the local actor.

Now, occasionally agents will scout (travel around the

nation), looking for a specific "someone." But the chances are slim even for kids living in the L.A. area who want to make it. The competition is fierce! As good as you think you are, there's someone else as good or better. I'm not trying to sound negative, but I *am* being realistic and telling you straight out how it really is.

Fourth, get some good photos. Every potential actor needs a composite or at least a good head shot. Find a professional photographer to capture you in several different poses. This will show your versatility. Quality photos can be expensive, but they're worth it. An agent can detect a professional photo from a snapshot without even blinking. Don't kid yourself. If Uncle Roy says he can take good pictures, don't assume they'll turn out like professional photos. There's a big difference!

Fifth, wait. Everyone wants to be an actor. Agents are literally *flooded* with composites and wannabes every single day. It's a tough business. Very few kids (though it looks like a lot from all the TV shows) are actually fortunate enough to be successful at acting.

Sixth, be willing to move. If you're serious about acting, though, you probably also have to be serious about moving. As I mentioned earlier, it'll be extremely hard to get cast in a Hollywood sitcom if you're living in South Dakota. How serious are you? Serious enough to move?

Obviously, this involves a lot more than simply packing up and heading West. If you're still a teen, it's probably impossible for you to leave, and you'll probably have to wait until you're an adult. Some families will temporarily move to southern California in hopes that their children will land a role on one of the new fall sitcoms.

If you are from out of state and decide to come to California, realize you have to pay moving expenses, apartment rent, and grocery bills. It sounds like actors make a lot, but the pay right now is actually less than it used to be.

A two-bedroom apartment in Southern California will

be *at least* $1,000 a month. Most are higher. In fact, the entire cost of living is slightly higher in California than in most places.

Every pilot season I see families from all around the nation coming in with their kids and renting an apartment . . . all in the hopes that their son or daughter will make it. And though some of them do make it, most go home disappointed. Again, I realize this sounds pessimistic, but I'm simply trying to be honest. It's tough. If you're determined, though, you can get agent information by calling the Screen Actors Guild: 213-954-1600.

A Few Names You Might Recognize

One of the most exciting things about professional acting is that I get to work with some terrific people. Even though I've already mentioned some of my coworkers on *Step,* I want to give you a closer look at who they really are. So let's start with my *Step by Step* family; then after that, I'll introduce you to some other actors, okay?

My "Family"

Sasha Mitchell (Cody Lambert)

Sasha has worked with Patrick Duffy before because several years ago they both played on the show *Dallas.*

Sasha's very generous. Once a year for the past four years, he's given the entire *Step* cast a catered lunch. This not only includes the actors, but the cameramen, producers—*everyone.* It's terrific! Last year we had barbecued ribs with all the fixings.

He's also done a few kick-boxing films and influenced

several of us in the cast to get involved in the sport. He's friendly with the whole cast, and it's fun to work with him.

Christine Lakin (Al Lambert)

Since Christine is still in school, we have classes together on the set. She does really well in school. She and Brandon Call join together in pulling some pretty good pranks from time to time. They used to gang up on Josh and me for some laughs.

Christine has given me some really neat Christmas gifts. She knows I'm a golf nut, and a few years ago she gave me a golf calculator. It's really cool. All the numbers are little golf balls, and it has little plastic trees and a sand trap on the top. The next year I received some fun video games for my Game Boy.

Christine likes the Atlanta Braves, and I'm always giving her a hard time about that. Whenever they lose, I tape the newspaper clippings on the outside of her dressing room door. When they win, she tapes the results on my door!

Angela Watson (Karen Foster)

I love to kid Angela by imitating her laugh. She'll start laughing at something funny on the set, and I'll start mimicking her, and she completely busts up! It's hilarious. She treats me like I'm really her little brother. We have a lot of fun together. We also talk a lot.

Angela also likes to sing—and she's pretty good! She even writes some of her own songs. And sports? Well, she loves the Florida Gators!

Brandon Call (J.T. Lambert)

Brandon has played some pretty good pranks on me! One time we got into a Silly String fight. He literally *saturated* me with green Silly String. I looked like a giant had blown his nose on me.

Sometimes I'll be saying my lines during a scene, and he'll be off to the side making faces at me, trying to get me to "break" in front of the camera. He's pretty funny. Brandon's also stable, though. He's a dependable guy, and the cast loves him.

Josh Byrne (Brendon Lambert)

Josh is a few years younger than me, but we have a ton of fun together. As I mentioned earlier, we go to school together on the set, and I help him with his math homework from time to time. We have P.E. together, and we love playing baseball and learning more about karate. Josh and I also enjoy goofing off together between scenes.

Staci Keanan (Dana Foster)

Since I've acted with Staci before, I've known her the longest. I love working with her. She's really a good actress—extremely versatile. Staci can play anything. She can also talk about anything. I wouldn't mind having her for my real sister.

Patrick Duffy (Frank Lambert)

Patrick is hilarious. He'll purposely do something funny on camera if someone messes up. His reactions are priceless.

But more than being funny—and more than being a fantastic actor—he's also a terrific example of what a family man should be like. It's obvious he's in love with his own family. He's always talking about his wife and kids. You can tell he's proud of them.

Patrick and Suzanne Somers are both very genuine and care a great deal about keeping their families a top priority. They haven't let the glitz and glamour of Hollywood turn them into phonies.

They're also very practical. Money doesn't dictate their

lives. They don't own big, fancy cars just for show. This tells me that they value the things in life that are more important than material possessions.

Patrick personally cares about the cast members and takes time for us if we need his help with something. A few years ago, I received a letter from a kook. I mean, this guy was a real psycho. Our family didn't know him, but he sent me a really sick letter—as in perverted, threatening, and filthy.

It really shook up my family. We didn't know if this guy was going to try to track us down or what. But my mom decided to talk to Patrick about it. He was all ears, and he gave us some great advice. I could tell that he wasn't just listening to be nice; he was genuinely concerned about me and my welfare. He put me in touch with the "Threat Management Department"—which is a special division of the police department. My mom talked with them and got some specific direction on what to do. But we wouldn't have known where to turn if Patrick hadn't taken time to help us.

Suzanne Somers (Carol Foster Lambert)

Suzanne's very professional when she's acting. Between scenes, though, she's hilarious; she occasionally makes blonde jokes about herself. And once in a while she'll do the "Chrissy" laugh and start snorting (she created that when she was starring in *Three's Company* several years ago). Suzanne's loved by everyone on the set.

She's also a good role model for us. She's devoted to her real family and places high value on being with them. As soon as her husband walks on the set, her entire face lights up. She smiles at everybody, but you can tell she's really in love with her husband.

Suzanne also works hard to make the kids in our cast

feel appreciated and loved. She hugs us a lot and tells us we're doing a good job. That means a lot—especially from a pro like her!

She grew up with an alcoholic father. A few years ago she wrote a one-woman show about her struggles with growing up in a dysfunctional family. She set the play to music and rented a theater in Hollywood. Then, as a Christmas gift, she invited the entire *Step* cast, crew, their families, and her close friends. There were about three hundred of us in attendance.

It was fantastic! Really, really touching. We were laughing one minute and crying the next. I was impressed first of all with her talent—she created the entire show! But I was also impacted by her willingness to be so open and vulnerable about her past, her hurt, and her determination to succeed in spite of all the hardships.

Suzanne Somers is amazing. I really admire her! She's also very approachable. Any one of us can go to her with our concerns, and she always makes the time to listen and to help us. I love her like a real mom.

More Friends

Here are some names you'll remember from *Beethoven, Beethoven's 2nd,* and other TV shows.

Charles Grodin (George Newton)

This guy is really outgoing. He knows no strangers. Since he and I both love sports, that's what we talked about between scenes. He has a great sense of dry humor. He was always making me laugh at something. The neat part about all this is that he knew just when to crack us up. He has an incredible sense of timing. Just when things would start to get tense, he'd loosen things up. He's always ready, and he's always professional.

Bonnie Hunt (Alice Newton)

Bonnie always makes me laugh. She was perfect for the part of our mom. Everyone loves her—she's everybody's favorite. Bonnie's never off somewhere by herself. She's always willing to talk and get to know the crew. She used to be a comedienne, so she's used to finding the punch line in everything. Even in a sad scene, she could always find something to make us laugh.

Nicholle Tom (Ryce Newton)

She treated me like a real brother. Since she likes sports, the two of us played catch between scenes. She's pretty good too! She also helped me with my schoolwork. I enjoyed acting with her.

Sarah Rose Karr (Emily Newton)

Sarah Rose is sweet. I tried to treat her like my own sister, because she's close to Bethany's age. She was fascinated with all the dogs.

Jaleel White (Steve Urkel on *Family Matters*)

Since our shows are both filmed at Warner Brothers Studios, we run into each other from time to time. He's the exact opposite in real life from the nerdy character he plays.

We've occasionally played basketball together on break between rehearsals. He's really a good athlete, and he's very serious about the game. Put a basketball in his hands and suddenly he's extremely focused on what he's doing. I admire his ability.

A few years ago I was privileged to get invited to Dyersville, Iowa, for a charity baseball game. We played on the field that was used for the movie *Field of Dreams*. I loved every minute of it!

We were fitted for old-fashioned uniforms, and we saw

the house that was used in the movie. The field is actually owned by two different families.

Other actors and athletes who participated in the game were Reggie Jackson, Bob Gibson, Candace Cameron (I helped her with her throw), Kelsey Grammer, and Bruce Boxleitner.

It's definitely an experience of a lifetime getting to know such a variety of professional people. Each person has his or her own way of doing things, but when the lights hit and the film begins to roll, all differences are put aside and we immediately become a team. That's what acting is all about.

Just for Fun!

Birthday   6-15-80
Height   5 feet 4 inches
Weight   106 pounds
Shampoo   Pert Plus
Deodorant   Speed Stick Regular
Cologne   Polo (Ralph Lauren)
Favorite TV show   *The Fresh Prince of Bel Air*

▼   ▼   ▼   ▼   ▼

I had a blast doing the voice of Eugene on
the "Hey, Arnold!" cartoon that debuted in
January of 1996. Cartoons are a fun
challenge. The whole process is fascinating—
you put everything you have into your voice
and try to project an entire range of
emotions through sound.

Favorite movies   *Aladdin, Hook,* and *The Lion King*

Favorite sports   Golf and baseball

Favorite holiday   Christmas

Favorite songs   "Breathless" by Kenny G and "Free at Last" by DC Talk

Favorite candy   Skittles

Favorite snack   Pringles chips

Favorite drink   Root beer

Worst illness   Chicken pox

Actors I'd love to be in a movie with   The two Toms—Tom Hanks and Tom Cruise

Actors I'd love to be on a future TV series with The actresses on *Friends* (I don't get to watch the show, but I *did* visit their set once and watched a live taping.)

Show I watched most as a child   I Love Lucy

▼   ▼   ▼   ▼   ▼

**When you see the lovable
St. Bernard, Beethoven, on screen,
you're actually looking at one of
eight lovable St. Bernards who were
used for the part. These adult dogs
were trained over a twenty-week
period to "play" the star.
Sixteen different puppies ranging in
sizes were used to portray Beethoven
as a tiny pup—when the film first
begins—and through his various
growing stages.**

Favorite relaxing pastimes   Playing golf, playing pool, and messing around with my computer

What I'd want if marooned on a desert island Golf clubs, a few buckets of balls, and my computer. I'd also request a sand wedge, so I could get out of the sand when playing golf.

The most important thing Mom has taught me Through Mom, I've learned to share my feelings, to stay genuine, and not get a big head.

Favorite subjects Math, science, P.E., and Spanish. I'd like to take French sometime, because I think it's a cool language and sounds so neat.

Subject I wish we didn't have English

Magazines I read regularly Golf Digest, Tennis, Breakaway

Favorite books October 1964 (a baseball book); *Rookie; The Michael Jordan Book; Buried Lies* (a golf book by Peter Jacobsen)

Place I'd most like to vacation in Hawaii

▼ ▼ ✔ ▼ ▼

I recently started taking flying lessons. (Pretty funny that I'm not driving yet but have soared through the air, huh?) The Santa Monica Airport offers a "Discovery Flight." They take you through some intensive instructions, and then they allow you to taxi the aircraft down the runway and take off! Of course, a licensed pilot is sitting right next to you the entire time, but he's not touching the controls.

Weirdest nightmare I dreamed I was a passenger on a plane, and the engines started acting up. So I got out of my seat and headed toward the cockpit to ask the pilots what was happening. When I opened the door to the cockpit, though, there were no pilots. It was empty! So I fastened myself into the pilot's chair and flew the plane to safety. (I really am interested in flying and would even like to be a pilot someday, so it was pretty funny that I dreamed this!)

What I'm most grateful for　　My family

The most important thing Dad has taught me　　The only time I'm allowed to burp in front of people is at home. Just kidding. He's taught me a lot about patience. Dad is very consistent. He's patient with each family member. I admire that about him. He's helping me learn that patience is a real virtue.

What my sister, Bethany, and I are　　Good friends. We don't always agree with each other, but I love her a lot. I know if our roles were reversed, I'd be jealous of her. But instead of being jealous of me, she's actually proud of me! Cool sister, huh? Besides all that, she's just really cute!

Who makes me laugh uncontrollably　　Actor Jerry Lewis

My dream car　　A Porsche . . . but I probably won't get one until I'm really old.

Instruments I play　　Flute, clarinet, and a little piano

What makes me cry　　When I see my mom choke up over a movie or something sad. Then I feel bad, too, and often start crying *with* her.

Whom I'd invite to dinner if I could invite any living person　　Peter Jacobsen, a pro golfer, writer, and musician

Whom I'd invite to dinner if I could invite anyone from history　　Jesus Christ and Babe Ruth

What's hanging on my walls　　Two lithographs of sports figures—Roger Clemens (pitcher for the Boston Red Sox) and Ricky Watters (running back for the San Francisco 49ers and 1,000-yard rusher for many years)—and a photo of me on the fourth hole at a Greensboro, N.C., golf course.

What I usually belt out in the shower   "Singin' in the Rain"

▼ ▼ ▼ ▼ ▼

When I filmed
Are You Afraid of the Dark?
(a Nickelodeon project), we shot in an actual
prison that hadn't been used in ten years.
Talk about creepy! We filmed at night, and
it was really weird finding old bird feathers
and a rat skeleton on the premises. Spooky.

Why I was last grounded   I was trying to spin a basketball on my finger, and in the process, I broke a light fixture.

What sport I'd be involved in if I could compete in the Olympics   Baseball. If they had golf, I'd play that too.

Age I'd choose if I could be one age forever   Eighteen years old. It's past puberty but before I have to make any huge decisions about my life, my lifemate, and my career.

What I'd do if I were given $10,000 in tax-free money   I'd arrange my own celebrity golf tournament for charity.

What I dream for my future   I'd like to become a pro golfer or baseball player. I'd also like to continue acting if people continue to think I have what it takes. I wouldn't mind dabbling in directing too.

My most treasured memory   When I was baptized at church. My best friend was baptized during the same service.

What I'd choose if I could wake up tomorrow having gained a new characteristic   Patience

My favorite family vacation   A cruise to the Caribbean

Place I'd choose if I had to live forever in another country   Canada

What I want inscribed on my tombstone   "He lived his life to the fullest."

▼   ▼   ▼   ▼   ▼

A few years ago, the Step cast got to film two episodes in Hawaii. It was great! We all went to Maui. Pretty cool perk, huh?

Something I'm not allowed to do   Chew gum on the set

Cartoon character I'd like to be   Taz

What I complain most about   Having to pick up my clothes and put them in the hamper

One thing I haven't done, but would love to do   Fly an airplane

Whom I'd choose to play me if a major motion picture were to be made of my life   Val Kilmer, Steve Martin, or Tom Hanks

The quality I value most in a friend   Honesty

Three things I will not do   Take God's name in vain, drink and drive, or curse

Favorite item of clothing   A starter jacket

Three things I'd miss most if I were moved to a primitive country   Running water, girls, and a toilet that flushes

▼   ▼   ▼   ▼   ▼

Step by Step went into syndication in September of '95—which means if you want to, you can watch every single night!

Three things I believe beyond all doubt   That my family loves me no matter what I do, that I'm going to heaven after I die, and that someday I'll get a hole in one.

What I need to do to improve myself   Start thinking before I do or say things

The thing I most look forward to about growing old Accomplishing my goals

What I'm frightened of Wasps, bees, hornets . . . anything that has a stinger—including shots

The last time I apologized Just a few hours ago. I accidentally ran headfirst into someone on the set.

What I'd do if I could read people's minds Read the mind of every girl who talks to me

The four things I'm most grateful for My family, my friends, my work, and my athletic abilities

Two of the most surprising gifts I've ever received Actress Nicollette Sheridan bought me a set of golf clubs, and my parents gave me a laptop computer.

Qualities of my grandparents that I'd like to have I want the care and love that my grandma has, and I want the generosity that my grandpa has.

Qualities that make a great guy/girl relationship Trust, honesty, and love

What I do when it comes to hugging Give out a lot. I'm definitely a good hugger. I learned it from my family.

▼　▼　▼　▼　▼

Filming Beethoven and Beethoven's 2nd aren't the only times I got to work with my furry friend. He once guest starred as "Mr. Fritz" on an episode of Step. It was great to be with him again!

The area in my life that I need more self-confidence in You guessed it—not being concerned about my height.

What I love Even though it's sort of a compliment to be recognized as the character I play, I really love it when people recognize me as "me."

What I most admire about my parent's marriage
They have an incredible amount of respect for each other. I also like the fact that they're both crazy about their kids. That definitely feels good!

What someone would find if he or she were to go through my personal trash can at the end of a week   Skittles wrappers, chewing gum, Kleenex, and old homework papers

The show I'd miss most if I stopped watching TV for one year   I Love Lucy reruns

The most beautiful thing I've ever seen   Sunsets in Hawaii

The most beautiful thing I've ever heard   Kenny G songs

The first thing I notice when meeting someone new
Their eyes

Three questions I'd love to ask God   Why did you make insects that sting? How does the sky turn pink during a sunset? Why do we die?

When I'm most happy   When I'm golfing and I'm playing well

My greatest weakness   Getting easily frustrated with myself when I don't do as well as I want to in sports

The type of person who brings out the best in me
Someone who loves to laugh, and someone who allows me to simply be "me" instead of expecting something more just because I'm an actor.

The most recent person I said "I love you" to   My mom

What I do when I'm angry   Roll my eyes

Whom I'd be willing to die for   My family

▼   ▼   ▼   ▼   ▼

Trainers searched ten states to find puppies adorable enough to follow in Beethoven's paw prints and play the roles of his "children." Over 250 of them were used, ranging in age from three weeks (playing newborns) to eight weeks (when they go on vacation with the Newton family).

Why so many stand-ins? The trainer explains it this way: "Three-week-old puppies are like infants," she says. "They have to nurse from their real mother four to five times during a shooting day. Then they have nap time and food elimination time. They're really too young to keep in front of the camera for very long."

So older puppies were used, but this brought another challenge. The older ones were filmable at seven weeks, but because they grew a pound a day, by eight and one-half weeks they were too old.

Beethoven and his canine costars had everything a dog could ask for. Since Saint Bernards are heavy-coated mountain dogs, they're most accustomed to cold weather. To make sure our four-footed friends were comfortable—and to keep them from panting—the stage temperature was kept in the low 60s.

When the cast had to fly to different locations for various shootings, the dogs were always flown first-class in specially constructed cages. And snacks? The doggie trailer was always stocked with favorite munchies like steaks and dog biscuits.

One More Thing . . .

Thanks for allowing me to share an inside peek at my life with you. I'm glad you took the time to read this book.

While we were finishing it, something changed in my family life. One of the worst things that can happen to a kid is happening to me. After much consideration, my parents decided to separate and get a divorce. As hard as it is on me and my family, I have to be realistic and know that life doesn't end here. And even though my parents might never be together again, I know they will always love me and be supportive of me. That's the most important thing to me.

As I have said, being an actor on a TV show doesn't mean I don't have to deal with some of the same difficult and scary things teens all over the world deal with. My sister and I have cried together, and I have moments of fear and anger at both my parents—not to mention feeling sorry for myself. It's going to be hard for all of us. But I have friends and other adults who are helping me through this because they've experienced it too. And I know from their advice that it won't always hurt as much as it does now. And I'm counting on that.

Everyone has his or her own opinion about stuff, and I won't know if you agree or disagree with what I've said unless you tell me. If you'd like to drop me a note, I'd love to hear from you. I'm sorry I can't answer each letter personally, but I'll try to answer some of them. I'd enjoy reading *your* opinion on the stuff we've talked about.

Chris Castile
Step by Step—ABC TV
2040 Avenue of the Stars
Century City, CA 90067

If you happen to visit Southern California, I hope you'll get tickets to the show. I'd love to see you sitting in our studio audience. Admission is free, but it would be best to contact Audience Unlimited ahead of time for tickets. Their number is: 1-800-339-7469. They're open Monday-Friday from 8:00 A.M. to 4:00 P.M.

About the Authors

Chris Castile is a high school student and professional actor. You've probably seen him in countless commercials, ABC's *Step by Step*, or *Beethoven* and *Beethoven's 2nd*.

Susie Shellenberger has authored fifteen books and is a former high school drama teacher. She currently resides in Colorado Springs and is the editor of *Brio* magazine, a monthly publication for teen girls.